A HAND BOOK ON SOCIOLOGY

TEKMAL SOLMANRAJ

To

GOD

dear and near ones

Contents

FOREWORD

In an increasingly complex world, understanding the fundamental principles of sociology is crucial for navigating the intricacies of human relationships, institutions, and societal structures. This comprehensive handbook on general principles of sociology provides a thorough exploration of the key concepts that shape our social world.

From the foundational aspects of kinship, marriage, and family to the complex dynamics of economic institutions, social stratification, and caste, this book offers a nuanced examination of the social forces that influence our lives. The inclusion of topics such as association, social change, and conflict further enriches our understanding of the ever-evolving nature of society.

This handbook serves as an invaluable resource for students, scholars, and anyone interested in gaining a deeper understanding of sociology. By providing a clear and concise overview of the field's core principles, this book empowers readers to engage with the social world in a more informed and thoughtful manner.

The authors' meticulous approach to explaining complex sociological concepts makes this book an essential guide for those seeking to explore the intricacies of human society. As we continue to navigate the challenges and opportunities of the modern world, this handbook provides a solid foundation for understanding the social dynamics that shape our lives.

Preface

Sociology, as a discipline, offers a unique lens through which to examine the complexities of human society. By exploring the social structures, institutions, and relationships that shape our lives, sociology provides valuable insights into the dynamics of power, inequality, and social change.

This handbook aims to provide a comprehensive introduction to the general principles of sociology, covering key concepts such as kinship, marriage, family, economic institutions, social stratification, caste, association, social change, and conflict. Through a clear and concise exploration of these topics, this book seeks to equip readers with a deeper understanding of the social world and its many complexities.

The motivation behind writing this book stems from a desire to make sociology accessible to a wider audience. By presenting complex concepts in an engaging and easy-to-understand manner, we hope to inspire readers to think critically about the social world and its many intricacies.

This book is designed to be a valuable resource for students, scholars, and anyone interested in gaining a better understanding of sociology. We believe that by exploring the principles of sociology, readers will gain a deeper appreciation for the complexities of human society and be better equipped to navigate the challenges and opportunities of the modern world.

Hope that this handbook will serve as a foundation for further exploration and discovery in the field of sociology, and we look forward to sharing our knowledge with readers.

ACKNOWLEDGEMENTS

We would like to extend our heartfelt gratitude to:

The Almighty: For guiding and inspiring us throughout this journey.

Our Parents: For their unwavering support, love, and encouragement.

Our Family Members: For their constant motivation and understanding.

Arshi (Best Friend): For being a source of comfort, encouragement, and valuable insights.

Brother Rohin and Family: For their love, support, and belief in us.

Their contributions, whether direct or indirect, have been invaluable in shaping this book. We are grateful for their presence in our lives and appreciate their impact on our work.

I
Introduction

Sociology plays a vital role in understanding human society and social behaviour. By studying sociology, we can gain valuable insights into social issues and develop effective solutions. Sociology helps us comprehend the complex dynamics of social relationships, institutions, and processes that shape our lives. It enables us to identify patterns and trends, understand social problems, and develop policies to address them.

The term "sociology" was coined by French philosopher Auguste Comte in 1839. The word originates from the Latin "Sociatas" (society) and Greek "Logos" (study of society). Sociology as a separate discipline began being taught in the United States in 1876, France in 1889, and Great Britain in 1907. Over time, sociology has evolved to become a distinct field of study, focusing on the scientific analysis of human social behaviour and relationships.

Sociology's scope is vast, encompassing the study of human interactions, relationships, and institutions. It examines the complex dynamics of social life, including the interplay between individuals, groups, and society as a whole. Sociology explores various aspects of social life, such as social structures, institutions, and processes. It also investigates the relationships between social and non-social factors, like culture, environment, and heredity.

Sociology can be defined as the scientific study of human social behaviour, relationships, and institutions. Various scholars have defined sociology in different ways, reflecting the field's complexity and diversity. According to Prof. Ginsberg, sociology is "the study of society, that is, of the web or tissue of human interactions and interrelations." Auguste Comte defined it as "a general study of whole society." Other notable definitions include those by Gittin and Gillin, Sorokin, Ogburn, H.M. Johnson, Ward, and H.P. Fairchild, each highlighting different aspects of the field.

Sociologists employ various research methods to study social phenomena, including observation, recording, classification, verification, and prediction. These methods enable sociologists to develop a deeper understanding of social issues and develop effective solutions. By using scientific methods, sociologists can collect and analyse data, identify patterns and trends, and draw meaningful conclusions.

Ultimately, sociology provides valuable insights into the complexities of human society and social behavior. It helps us develop a nuanced understanding of social issues and develop effective strategies to address them. Through its focus on human interactions, relationships, and institutions, sociology offers a unique perspective on the social world and our place within it.

The Significance of Sociology

Sociology plays a vital role in understanding human society and social behaviour. By studying sociology, we can gain valuable insights into social issues and develop effective solutions. Sociology helps us comprehend the complex dynamics of social relationships, institutions, and processes that shape our lives. It enables us to identify patterns and trends, understand social problems, and develop policies to address them.

The Origin of Sociology

The term "sociology" was coined by French philosopher Auguste Comte in 1839. The word originates from the Latin "Sociatas" (society) and Greek "Logos" (study of society). Sociology as a separate discipline began being taught in the United States in 1876, France in

1889, and Great Britain in 1907. Over time, sociology has evolved to become a distinct field of study, focusing on the scientific analysis of human social behavior and relationships.

The Scope of Sociology

Sociology's scope is vast, encompassing the study of human interactions, relationships, and institutions. It examines the complex dynamics of social life, including the interplay between individuals, groups, and society as a whole. Sociology explores various aspects of social life, such as social structures, institutions, and processes. It also investigates the relationships between social and non-social factors, like culture, environment, and heredity.

Defining Sociology

Sociology can be defined as the scientific study of human social behavior, relationships, and institutions. Various scholars have defined sociology in different ways, reflecting the field's complexity and diversity. According to Prof. Ginsberg, sociology is "the study of society, that is, of the web or tissue of human interactions and interrelations." Auguste Comte defined it as "a general study of whole society." Other notable definitions include those by Gittin and Gillin, Sorokin, Ogburn, H.M. Johnson, Ward, and H.P. Fairchild, each highlighting different aspects of the field.

The definitions stated above clearly indicate that different sociologists have defined Sociology in different ways. Some of the definitions of other sociologists as also given below to understand the subject adequately :

W.F. Ogburn-"Sociology is a body of learning about society. It is a description of ways to make society better. It is social ethics, a social philosophy. Generally, however, it is defined as a science of society."

Park and Burgess-"Sociology is the science of collective behaviour."

Von Wiese "Sociology is a special social science, concentrating on inter-human behaviour."

G.A. Lundberg "Sociology is a body of related generalizations about human social behaviour arrived at by scientific method."

M.E. Jones "The Chief interest of sociology is the people the ideas, the customs, the other distinctively human phenomena which surround man and influence him, and which are, therefore, part of his environment. Sociology also devotes some attention to certain aspects of the geographical environment and to some natural as contrasted with human phenomena, but this interest is secondary to its preoccupation with human beings and the products of human life in association. Our general field of study is man as he is related to other men and to the creation of other man which surround him."

Kimball Young-"Sociology deals with the behaviour of men in groups."

Reuter-"The purpose of Sociology is to establish a body of valid principles, a fund of objective knowledge that will make possible the direction and control of social and human reality."

Giddings-"Sociology is an attempt to account for the origin, growth, structure and activities of society by the operation of physical causes working together in the process of evolution."

Tonnies "Sociology is on the whole the theory of human living together."

MacIver and Page "Sociology seeks to discover the principles of cohesion and of order within the social structure, the ways in which it roots and within grows an environment, the moving equilibrium of changing structure and changing environments, the main trends of the incessant change the forces which determine its direction at any time and so on."

Robert Biersted-"Sociology seeks general laws or principles about human interactions and association, about the nature, form, content and structure of human groups and societies."

Simmel "Sociology asks what happens to men and by what rules they behave not in so far as they unfold their undesirable individual existences in their totalities, but in so far as they form groups and are determined by their existence because of interaction."

Young and Mack-"Sociology is the scientific study of the social aspects of human life."

John F. Cuber-"Sociology may be defined as a body of scientific knowledge about human relationships."

Kingsly Davis-"Sociology is the study of social life."

Emile Durkheim-"Sociology is a study of collective representation."

E.S. Bogardus-"Sociology may be defined as the study of the ways in which special experiences function in developing, maturing and repressing human beings through inter-personal stimulation

Max Weber-"Sociology is the science which attempts the interpretive understanding of social action."

T. Abel "Sociology is the scientific study of social relationships, their variety, their forms, whatever affects them and whatever they affect." Arthur Fairbanks "Sociology is the name applied to somewhat inchoate mass of materials which embodies our knowledge of society." Arnold Green-"Sociology is the synthesizing and generalising science of man in all his social relationships."

John W. Bennet - "Sociology is the science of the structure and functions of social life."

G. Duncan Mitchell-"Sociology is a science for scientific social development."

Sociology provides a comprehensive understanding of human life in relation to others, encompassing interactions, associations, and influences. It employs a scientific and historical approach to study social phenomena, considering both social and non-social factors. Sociology has become a crucial branch of knowledge, guiding individuals toward a better life by examining various aspects, including:

- Social problems
- Human ecology
- Race and culture
- Collective behaviour
- Social institutions
- Socialization of human wants and means of satisfaction

Sociology can be viewed in multiple ways:

- As a science of society
- As a science of social relationships
- As the study of social life
- As the study of human behaviour in groups
- As the study of social action
- As the study of forms of social relationships
- As the study of social groups or social systems

These perspectives highlight sociology's diverse scope and its role in understanding complex social dynamics.

Sociology has several key characteristics that establish its scientific nature. These characteristics not only define the discipline but also distinguish it from other fields of study.

1. Sociology is a Social Science

Sociology studies human behavior in society, focusing on the interactions and relationships between individuals, groups, and institutions. This distinguishes it from natural sciences, which examine inanimate phenomena. As a social science, sociology seeks to understand the complexities of human social behavior, social structures, and institutions.

2. Sociology is a Positive Science

Sociology adopts a realistic approach, studying social phenomena as they exist, rather than focusing on what ought to be. This means that sociologists aim to describe and explain social phenomena objectively, without imposing their own values or biases. By doing so, sociology provides a nuanced understanding of social issues and problems.

3. Sociology is Both Pure and Applied Science

Sociology encompasses both theoretical and practical aspects, making it a comprehensive field that informs both understanding and action. As a pure science, sociology seeks to develop and test theories about social phenomena. As an applied science, sociology uses this knowledge to address practical problems and improve society. This dual nature of sociology makes it a valuable tool for policymakers, practitioners, and researchers.

4. Sociology is an Abstract Science

Sociology examines social phenomena in general, rather than concrete, specific instances. This means that sociologists aim to identify patterns and principles that apply to a wide range of social contexts. By abstracting from specific cases, sociology provides a deeper understanding of social phenomena and their underlying structures and processes.

5. Sociology is a Science of Generalization

Sociology seeks to identify patterns and principles applicable to various social contexts, distinguishing it from other social sciences. By generalizing from specific cases, sociology provides a broader understanding of social phenomena and their underlying causes. This enables sociologists to develop theories and models that can be applied to different social settings.

6. Sociology is a Rational Empirical Science

Sociology combines logical reasoning with empirical data collection and analysis to understand social phenomena. Sociologists use a range of research methods, including surveys, interviews, and observations, to collect data and test hypotheses. By combining rational inquiry with empirical evidence, sociology provides a robust understanding of social phenomena.

7. Sociology is a General Science

Sociology's broad scope and general approach set it apart from other social sciences, which often focus on specific aspects of society. Sociology examines social phenomena in a holistic manner, considering the complex interplay between different social factors. This general approach enables sociologists to develop a comprehensive understanding of social systems and processes.

The scope of sociology

The scope of sociology is a topic of ongoing debate among sociologists, with two main schools of thought: the Specialistic or Formal School and the Synthetic School.

Specialistic or Formal School

This school advocates for a narrow scope, focusing on the study of social relationships, their forms, and abstract nature. Proponents like Max Weber, George Simmel, and Von Wiese believe that sociology should concentrate on understanding the underlying structures and patterns of social relationships. They argue that by studying the forms of social relationships, sociologists can identify universal principles and mechanisms that shape human behavior.

The formalistic approach

The formalistic approach has been influential in shaping the field of sociology, particularly in the areas of social network analysis and social structure. However, critics argue that this approach has several limitations.

Criticisms of the Formalistic School

Narrowing the scope of sociology: Critics argue that the formalistic school's focus on abstract forms of social relationships neglects the concrete content of social life. By ignoring the specific contexts and meanings that people attach to their relationships, sociologists may miss important insights into human behavior.

Separating form from content: The formalistic school's attempt to separate the form of social relationships from their content is seen as artificial and impractical. Social forms are often shaped by their content, and ignoring this can lead to oversimplification or misinterpretation of social phenomena.

Impracticality of pure sociology: Critics argue that the idea of a "pure" sociology, uncontaminated by other disciplines, is unrealistic. Sociology is inherently interdisciplinary, and attempts to isolate it from other fields can lead to a lack of nuance and depth in understanding social phenomena.

Synthetic School

The Synthetic School, on the other hand, advocates for a broader scope, encompassing the study of human society as a whole. Supporters like Durkheim, Hobhouse, and Sorokin believe that sociology should aim to understand the complex interplay between different aspects of society, including economic, political, cultural, and social factors.

By taking a more holistic approach, sociologists can gain a deeper understanding of how social systems function and how they shape individual behavior. The Synthetic School's approach recognizes that social phenomena are often interconnected and that understanding these relationships is essential for developing effective social policies.

Advantages of the Synthetic School

Comprehensive understanding: The Synthetic School's approach provides a more comprehensive understanding of social phenomena, taking into account the complex interplay between different factors.

Interdisciplinary insights: By drawing on insights from multiple disciplines, sociologists can develop a more nuanced understanding of social issues and develop more effective solutions.

Contextual understanding: The Synthetic School's focus on concrete social contexts allows sociologists to understand how social phenomena are shaped by specific historical, cultural, and economic conditions.

Division of Sociology

Sociology can be divided into several branches or divisions, depending on the perspective of the sociologist. According to Durkheim, sociology has three principal divisions:

Sociology exhibits several characteristics that establish it as a scientific discipline:

1. Use of Scientific Methods

Sociology employs various scientific methods, including experiments, sociometry scales, schedules, questionnaires, interviews, and case histories. These methods involve systematic observation, recording, classification, verification, and prediction, mirroring the scientific approach used in other disciplines.

2. Focus on Facts

Sociologists study society and social institutions based on empirical evidence, relying on available facts and data to develop generalizations. This focus on factual information ensures that sociological findings are grounded in reality.

3. Universality of Principles

Sociological principles are considered universal, meaning their validity can be examined and verified by anyone. Under similar circumstances, sociological laws and principles are expected to hold true, regardless of time or place.

4. Cause-and-Effect Relationships

Sociology explores the relationships between causes and effects, seeking to understand how social phenomena are interconnected. By examining these relationships, sociologists can identify patterns and develop explanations for social processes and relationships.

5. Predictive Power

Sociologists can make informed predictions about social phenomena based on their analysis of cause-and-effect relationships and available data. This predictive power enables sociologists to anticipate potential outcomes and develop strategies for addressing social issues.

These characteristics demonstrate that sociology shares many features with other scientific disciplines, supporting its status as a science.

Objections to Sociology as a Science

Some critics argue that sociology lacks the characteristics of a pure or perfect science. The following points are raised:

1. Lack of Experimentation

Sociologists face significant challenges in conducting experiments due to the complexity and variability of society. Unlike natural sciences, sociology cannot isolate and analyze elements in a controlled laboratory setting. This limitation makes it difficult to establish cause-and-effect relationships and to test hypotheses with precision.

Some argue that without experimentation, sociology cannot be considered a science. Sprott remarks, "If you cannot experiment, if you cannot measure, if you cannot establish broad unifying hypotheses and if you cannot be confident in your social engineering, you cannot be said to be engaged in scientific study at all."

However, others counter that experimentation is not the only defining feature of science. Sociology can still employ scientific methods, such as observation, recording, and analysis, to develop and test theories.

2. Lack of Objectivity

Sociologists may struggle to maintain objectivity due to:

- Difficulty in measuring sentiments and emotions: Quantifying human feelings and experiences can be challenging. Sociologists may need to rely on qualitative methods, such as interviews and observations, which can be subjective.

- Personal biases and prejudices: Sociologists, as human beings, may bring their own biases and perspectives to their research. This can influence their interpretation of data and their conclusions.

Maintaining objectivity in sociology can be difficult, especially when studying sensitive or controversial topics. Sociologists may face public hostility or criticism if their findings are perceived as challenging dominant narratives or power structures.

3. Lack of Reactivity and Precision

Sociology's laws and conclusions may not be expressed in precise terms, and predictions may not always come true. This lack of precision and reactivity raises questions about sociology's scientific status.

Sociological phenomena are often complex and influenced by multiple factors, making it challenging to develop precise laws or predictions. However, this does not mean that sociology cannot provide valuable insights into human society and behavior.

Relationship with Other Sciences

Sociology has close relationships with other social sciences, including anthropology, economics, political science, and social psychology. These disciplines share a common goal of scientifically exploring social behavior and its products.

Commonalities and Differences

While each social science has its unique focus and approach, they often overlap and complement one another. For instance:

- Common object of study: Different sciences may study the same object from various perspectives, such as the study of human behavior in sociology, psychology, and anthropology.

- Interdisciplinary approaches: Sciences like social psychology draw on insights from multiple disciplines, including sociology and psychology.

- Shared methodologies: Many social sciences employ similar research methods, such as surveys, interviews, and observations.

Sociology and Economics

Sociology and economics are closely related, as economic phenomena are often shaped by social factors. Key points include:

- Overlap between economic and social activity: Economic actions are influenced by social structures, institutions, and relationships.

- Mutual influence: Sociology informs economics by providing insights into social context, while economics contributes to sociology by highlighting economic factors that shape social behavior.

- Shared concerns: Both sociology and economics study issues like inequality, poverty, and social change.

- Economic sociology: This subfield examines the social causes and consequences of economic phenomena.

Differences between sociology and economics include:

- Focus: Sociology studies social aspects of economic activities, while economics focuses on the economic process and mechanisms of production and distribution.

- Scope: Sociology has a broader scope, encompassing various aspects of social life, whereas economics is primarily concerned with economic activities.

- Methodology: Economics often employs quantitative methods, while sociology uses a range of qualitative and quantitative approaches.

- Theoretical perspectives: Sociology and economics draw on different theoretical frameworks, such as conflict theory and neoclassical economics.

Sociology and History

Sociology and history are interconnected, as historical context is essential for understanding social phenomena. Key points include:

- Historical background: Sociology draws on historical data to study social institutions and compare them across time and societies.

- Mutual dependence: History and sociology inform each other, with history providing context for sociological analysis and sociology offering insights into social structures and relationships.

- Comparative analysis: Sociologists use historical data to compare social phenomena across different time periods and societies.

- Social change: Both sociology and history study social change and its impact on societies.

Differences between sociology and history include:

- Focus: History describes unique events, while sociology produces generalizations about social phenomena.

- Attitude: History deals with concrete events, whereas sociology studies abstract social relationships.

- Methodology: History often focuses on narrative and descriptive approaches, while sociology employs a range of qualitative and quantitative methods.

- Theoretical frameworks: Sociology and history draw on different theoretical frameworks, such as structural functionalism and historical materialism.

Sociology and Psychology

Sociology and psychology are linked, as individual mental processes and behaviors are shaped by social factors. Key points include:

- Social psychology: This interdisciplinary field draws on insights from sociology and psychology to study human behavior in social contexts.

- Mutual influence: Sociology informs psychology by providing insights into social structures and relationships, while psychology contributes to sociology by highlighting individual-level factors that shape social behavior.

- Shared concerns: Both sociology and psychology study issues like social influence, group dynamics, and human behavior.

- Social cognition: Sociologists and psychologists examine how people perceive, process, and respond to social information.

The relationship between sociology and psychology is evident in areas like:

- Public opinion: Sociologists and psychologists study how public opinion is formed and influenced by social factors.

- Mob behavior: Both disciplines examine the social and psychological factors that contribute to collective behavior.

- Social movements: Sociologists and psychologists investigate the social and psychological dynamics of social movements and collective action.

- Mental health: Sociology and psychology intersect in the study of mental health, including the social causes and consequences of mental illness.

II

Social Norms and Values

Social norms and values are the foundation of any society, providing a framework for understanding and regulating human behavior. They are the unwritten rules that govern our interactions with others, shaping our attitudes, beliefs, and actions. Social norms are based on values, which are fundamental principles that guide our behavior and decision-making. These norms and values are essential for maintaining social order, promoting cooperation, and fostering a sense of community.

In every society, social norms play a crucial role in regulating the behavior of individuals and groups. They provide a shared understanding of what is considered acceptable and unacceptable behavior, helping to prevent conflicts and promote social cohesion. Norms can be informal, such as customs and traditions, or formal, such as laws and regulations. They can be enforced through social sanctions, such as approval or disapproval, or through more formal mechanisms, such as punishment or reward.

The study of social norms and values is important for understanding how societies function and how individuals interact with each other. By examining the norms and values that underlie social behavior, we can gain insights into the ways in which societies maintain order, promote cooperation, and address social problems.

Definition of Norms

According to Secord and Backman, "A norm is a standard of behavioral expectation shared by group members against which the validity of perceptions is judged and the appropriateness of feeling and behavior is evaluated." Norms set patterns that limit individual behavior, allowing individuals to seek alternate ways to achieve their goals within established boundaries, as noted by Broom and Selznick.

Types of Norms

There are two types of norms in every society:

- Ideal Norms: These are norms that a society sets forth for its members, expecting them to be accepted and obeyed. However, these norms may be unattainable for some individuals.

- Practical Norms: These are norms that are expected to be followed and practiced by members of society. They are considered achievable and are strictly enforced.

Role of Norms in Society

Norms play a crucial role in shaping social behavior and providing a sense of cohesion and order in society. By understanding and adhering to norms, individuals can navigate social situations effectively and contribute to the overall well-being of their community.

Characteristics of Social Norms

Social norms have several key characteristics that shape their role in society. These characteristics include:

1. Written and Unwritten: Social norms can be both written (laws) and unwritten (traditions, customs, fashions).

2. Cultural Relationship: Social norms are closely tied to the cultural pattern of a particular society, varying according to factors like economic status.

3. Foundation of Society: Norms are based on social behaviors that govern or form the foundation of society, helping individuals

distinguish between right and wrong.

4. Formation and Influence: Norms guide and influence behavior, and are also formed and established by individuals through social interaction.

5. Sense of Duty: Norms are closely related to an individual's sense of duty, compelling them to observe and follow these norms.

6. Presentation of New Behaviors: Norms can present new types of behavior, which individuals may accept or reject.

7. Conservatism: Most social norms, except for fashions and laws, tend to be conservative, preserving traditional practices and values.

8. Gradual Development: Norms develop slowly and gradually through social interaction, as members of society accept and internalize them over time.

9. Contextual Operability: Social norms operative in one system may not be applicable in another, reflecting differences in cultural, religious, or social contexts.

10. Relevance to Status and Occupation: Norms often vary according to an individual's sex, occupation, and status, with different expectations for those in different positions.

11. Control over Behavior: Social norms play a crucial role in controlling social behavior and conduct, shaping individual actions and decisions.

12. Adoption of Group Attitude: Norms can compel individuals to change their attitudes and adopt group attitudes, promoting conformity and social cohesion.

13. Situational Limitations: Social norms may not be suitable for all situations or conditions, requiring flexibility and adaptability.

14. Group-Specific: Norms can vary from group to group, depending on the purpose and context of the group.

These characteristics highlight the complex and multifaceted nature of social norms, which play a vital role in shaping individual behavior and social interactions.

Social norms

are not formed overnight, but rather are the result of a gradual development shaped by various factors. These factors, which contribute to the growth and development of social norms, can be categorized into four main sources: customs and traditions, social institutions, cultural values, and social interaction. Customs and traditions reflect the values and practices of a society, while social institutions like family, education, and religion provide a framework for socialization. Cultural values define what is considered acceptable and unacceptable behavior, and social interaction allows individuals to learn and internalize norms through communication and socialization. These sources interact and influence one another, shaping the complex nature of social norms.

Biological Source of Norms

The idea that humans are naturally inclined to follow norms is a perspective shared by some social thinkers. While it's not entirely accurate to attribute norm development solely to biology, as other factors also play a role, it's undeniable that social norms often reflect human instincts and biological traits. These innate tendencies can shape individual behavior and influence the norms that govern social interactions, highlighting the complex interplay between biology and environment in shaping human social behavior.

Religious and Moral Base of Social Norms

The relationship between social norms, religion, and morality is complex and multifaceted. Some social thinkers believe that social norms are shaped by religious and moral values, suggesting that these values provide a foundation for understanding right and wrong. However, this perspective is not entirely accurate, as social norms are influenced by a wide range of factors, including cultural, historical, and social contexts.

In reality, religion and morals are components of social norms, and they are often influenced by the values and norms of a society. This means that religious and moral values can shape social norms, but they are also shaped by them. For example, a society's norms around issues like equality and justice can influence the way that religious and moral values are interpreted and applied.

Ultimately, the relationship between social norms, religion, and morality is dynamic and reciprocal, with each influencing the other in complex ways. Understanding this relationship is essential for grasping the ways in which social norms are formed and evolve over time.

Social Base of Norms

The social base of norms theory posits that social norms emerge from the very fabric of society itself. According to this perspective, social norms are born out of the capacity of humans to learn and communicate symbolically. Society demands the existence of social norms to function and maintain order, and therefore, norms are an inherent part of social life. This theory highlights the idea that social norms are not imposed from outside, but rather they arise from the interactions and relationships within society.

Evolutionary Base of Social Norms

The evolutionary base of social norms suggests that norms have developed gradually over time, in tandem with the growth and development of society. According to this perspective, social norms have emerged as a way to help societies adapt to their environment and ensure their survival. As societies have evolved, so too have the norms that govern behavior, reflecting the changing needs and circumstances of the community. This theory provides a dynamic understanding of social norms, highlighting their role in facilitating social adjustment and promoting collective well-being.

Formation and Kinds of Social Norms

The formation of social norms is a complex process that has been studied through various experiments and research. These studies have led to a deeper understanding of how norms are formed and the different types of norms that exist.

Individual Norms

Individual norms are personal standards that individuals develop to guide their behavior in various situations. These norms are shaped by an individual's experiences, values, and interactions with others. They help individuals adjust to society and navigate social interactions. Individual norms can vary widely from person to person, reflecting the unique characteristics and perspectives of each individual.

Social Norms

Social norms, on the other hand, are shared expectations and standards that govern behavior within a group or society. They emerge from the tendency of individuals to conform to societal expectations and behave in similar ways. Social norms facilitate effective behavior and adjustment to the environment, and are widely accepted as good social norms. They play a crucial role in shaping behavior and promoting social cohesion.

Key Differences

The key difference between individual norms and social norms is that individual norms are personal and specific to each individual, while social norms are shared and apply to a larger group or society. Social norms are often more influential in shaping behavior, as individuals tend to conform to the expectations of their social group.

Importance of Social Norms

Social norms are essential for maintaining social order and promoting cooperation within a group or society. They provide a common understanding of what is considered acceptable and unacceptable behavior, helping to guide individual behavior and promote social cohesion. By understanding social norms, we can better appreciate the complex dynamics of social interaction and the ways in which individuals and groups shape and are shaped by their social environment.

Assimilation and Modification of social norms.-

Assimilation and modification of social norms is a complex process. When individuals internalize social norms, they become an integral part of their behavior, making it challenging to modify them. Once norms are deeply ingrained, they can become automatic and habitual. For instance, a child learns norms from their parents and environment, and once these norms are internalized, changing them can be difficult. People often accept social norms without resistance, which can contribute to their persistence. This acceptance can stem from socialization, cultural influence, and fear of social exclusion. As a result, modifying social norms requires a thoughtful and multi-faceted approach that takes into account the complexities of human behavior and social influence.

The acceptance of social norms can be attributed to several factors, including fear of social exclusion, desire for social approval, cultural tradition, socialization, and sense of belonging. Individuals often conform to social norms to avoid rejection or ridicule, seeking instead social approval and acceptance. Social norms deeply rooted in cultural traditions and values seem natural and acceptable, while socialization from a young age makes these norms an integral part of behavior. Ultimately, conforming to social norms gives individuals a sense of belonging to a group or community, further solidifying their acceptance and adherence.

Factors Influencing Acceptance of Social Norms

The acceptance of social norms is a multifaceted phenomenon, influenced by various factors that shape individual behavior and societal interactions. Understanding these factors is crucial for grasping why social norms are widely accepted and followed.

1. Prestige Suggestion

Prestige suggestion plays a significant role in the acceptance of social norms. When respected members of society, such as parents, community leaders, or influential figures, endorse certain norms, others are more likely to follow. This is particularly evident in the way children often adopt the norms and values of their parents or caregivers without question. The prestige associated with these figures lends credibility to the norms, making them more acceptable and desirable.

2. Ignorance About Other Norms

In some cases, individuals may adhere to social norms simply because they are unaware of alternative norms or practices. This is more common in less developed or isolated societies where exposure to diverse perspectives and norms is limited. However, even in more developed and educated societies, individuals may still follow norms without critically evaluating them, often due to a lack of awareness about other possibilities.

3. Tendency of Social Conformity

The tendency towards social conformity is a powerful force in shaping behavior. Individuals often conform to societal norms to avoid standing out or facing social exclusion. This desire to fit in and be accepted by others can lead people to adopt and follow norms without questioning their validity or relevance. Social conformity can be driven by a need for social approval and a fear of being ostracized or ridiculed.

4. Fear of Social Disapproval

Fear of social disapproval is another significant factor influencing the acceptance of social norms. Individuals often seek approval and acceptance from their community, and deviating from established norms can lead to disapproval or even punishment. This fear can motivate people to conform to societal expectations, even if they personally disagree with the norms. The desire for social approval and the avoidance of disapproval can be a strong motivator for adhering to social norms.

Implications

These factors highlight the complex interplay between individual behavior and societal influences. Understanding the reasons behind the acceptance of social norms can provide insights into how norms are formed, maintained, and changed over time. By recognizing the role of prestige suggestion, ignorance about other norms, social conformity, and fear of social disapproval, we can better appreciate the dynamics of social norm acceptance and its impact on individual and collective behavior.

Values are fundamental principles that serve as higher-order norms, guiding human behavior and decision-making. They provide standards for evaluating choices and actions, and express moral imperatives that shape individual and collective conduct. Social values are cultural standards that define what is desirable and good for organized social life, providing meaning and legitimacy to social arrangements and behavior.

These values vary across societies, reflecting unique cultural, historical, and social contexts. Many norms can be seen as reflections of values, with a single value being expressed through multiple norms and practices. For instance, the value of human life is reflected in safety regulations, norms for resolving disputes, hygiene standards, and rules governing transportation.

Shared values are essential for social cohesion and cooperation, enabling individuals to work together towards common goals and maintain social order. Without shared values, individuals may pursue conflicting goals, leading to disorder and disruption. Therefore, shared norms and values are crucial for an ordered and stable society, providing a foundation for cooperation, mutual understanding, and collective well-being.

Distinction Between Individual and Social Values

Individual values are personal and self-centered, focusing on what benefits the individual alone, such as wealth, power, or prestige. In contrast, social values prioritize the welfare and well-being of others, reflecting a concern for the collective good. Social values are internalized within an individual's personality through the process of socialization, influencing their thoughts, feelings, and behaviors. By integrating social values, individuals develop a sense of responsibility towards others, which guides their actions and decisions. This distinction highlights the importance of social values in shaping prosocial behavior and promoting the greater good.

III

Folk ways

Folkways are the customary ways of thinking, feeling, and behaving within a society, often followed without strict enforcement. These informal norms are not crucial for the group's welfare, but violating them may result in social ridicule or gossip. Folkways vary across societies and are shaped by tradition, repetition, and collective behavior. They include conventions, etiquette, and modes of behavior that individuals follow in their daily lives.

The concept of folkways was first introduced by William Graham Sumner, who described them as the product of frequent repetition of petty acts by many individuals acting in concert or facing similar needs. Folkways emerge unconsciously in a group and are recognized or accepted ways of behaving in society. They are simple habits of action common to group members, standardized and persisting due to traditional sanctions.

Folkways play a significant role in shaping individual behavior and reflecting collective values and traditions. They provide a sense of belonging and identity to group members and help to maintain social order and cohesion. Understanding folkways provides insight into the complexities of social norms and cultural variation, highlighting their importance in everyday life.

Moreover, folkways are not static and can change over time as societal values and norms evolve. They can also vary within different subgroups of a society, reflecting the diversity of cultural practices and traditions. By studying folkways, we can gain a deeper understanding of how social norms are formed, maintained, and transmitted across generations.

In conclusion, folkways are an integral part of social life, influencing individual behavior and shaping collective identity. They are a vital aspect of cultural heritage, reflecting the values, traditions, and customs of a society. By examining folkways, we can better appreciate the complexities of social behavior and the importance of cultural understanding in an increasingly diverse world.

Characteristics of Folkways

Folkways have several distinct characteristics that shape their nature and role in society. These characteristics include:

1. Spontaneous Growth

Folkways develop naturally and standardly without conscious or deliberate attempts. They emerge from the collective behavior and practices of individuals within a society, often evolving over time through repetition and tradition.

2. Social Objective

Folkways are based on social aims and objectives, serving a specific purpose within the community. They are designed to meet the needs and expectations of the group, providing a framework for social interaction and cooperation.

3. Social Control and Regulation

Folkways enjoy social sanction and regulate the behavior of society members. They provide a framework for acceptable behavior and influence individual actions, helping to maintain social order and cohesion.

4. Variation Across Societies

Folkways differ from society to society, reflecting the unique cultural, social, and economic conditions of each community. There is no universal standard for folkways, and what is considered acceptable in one society may not be in another.

5. No Moral Implications

Folkways are not moral standards or values. Violating folkways may result in social disapproval or blame, but it is not considered a breach of moral codes. Instead, folkways are more related to social etiquette and conventions.

Implications of Folkways

Understanding the characteristics of folkways is essential for appreciating their role in shaping social behavior and cultural practices. Folkways play a significant part in:

- Shaping individual behavior and social interaction

- Maintaining social order and cohesion

- Reflecting the unique cultural and social context of a community

- Influencing social norms and values

By recognizing the characteristics of folkways, we can better navigate the complexities of social behavior and cultural diversity, fostering greater understanding and cooperation within and across societies.

IV
Mores

Mores are norms that are considered crucial for the well-being of society, and their violation leads to strong social disapproval. Coined by William Graham Sumner, the term "mores" refers to those norms that are of great significance and are essential for maintaining social order and stability. Mores emerge when folkways become attached to group welfare and are considered vital for society's well-being.

Mores are characterized by their importance to society's welfare, and violating them results in severe social disapproval and punishment. Conformity to mores, on the other hand, brings social approval and recognition. Various sociologists have defined mores, highlighting their significance in shaping social behavior and promoting collective welfare.

Mores are distinct from folkways in that they are more rigid and serious, often dealing with fundamental aspects of social life such as morality, ethics, and justice. They are not simply matters of etiquette or custom, but rather essential norms that underpin the functioning of society.

The significance of mores lies in their ability to promote social cohesion, order, and stability. By adhering to mores, individuals demonstrate their commitment to the well-being of society and their willingness to conform to its norms. This, in turn, helps to build trust, cooperation, and a sense of community among members of society.

In conclusion, mores play a vital role in shaping social behavior and promoting collective welfare. They are essential norms that underpin the functioning of society, and their violation can have serious consequences. By understanding mores, we can gain insight into the complex dynamics of social norms and their impact on individual and collective behavior.

Characteristics of Mores

Mores have distinct characteristics that shape their role in society. These characteristics include:

1. Concept of Group Welfare

Mores are attached to the welfare of the group or society, and this element converts folkways into mores. The emphasis on group welfare highlights the importance of collective well-being and the role of mores in promoting it.

2. Determine Mode of Behavior

Mores determine modes of day-to-day behavior as social beings, influencing interactions with others, such as behavior towards parents and elder individuals. By shaping behavior, mores help maintain social order and promote harmony.

3. Helpful in Social Adjustment

Mores serve as guides for social behavior, based on societal values and attitudes, facilitating social adjustment and cohesion. By following mores, individuals can navigate complex social situations and build strong relationships.

4. Uniformity in Social Life

Mores bring uniformity to social behavior, as their violation results in punishment, encouraging conformity to prescribed standards. This uniformity helps maintain social stability and predictability.

5. Instrumental in Social Change

Mores can also drive social change, as prolonged persistence can lead to restlessness and efforts to bring about change. By challenging outdated or unjust mores, individuals and groups can work towards creating a more just and equitable society.

Implications of Mores

Understanding the characteristics of mores is essential for appreciating their role in shaping social behavior and promoting collective welfare. Mores play a vital part in:

- Maintaining social order and stability
- Promoting social cohesion and harmony
- Guiding individual behavior and decision-making
- Shaping cultural values and attitudes
- Driving social change and progress

By recognizing the significance of mores, we can better navigate the complexities of social norms and work towards creating a more just and harmonious society.

Distinction between Folkways and Mores

Folkways and mores are both social norms, but they differ in their significance, impact, and characteristics. The key distinctions between folkways and mores are:

1. Generality

- Folkways are more general and informal, governing everyday behavior, such as customs, traditions, and etiquette.

- Mores are less general and more specific, dealing with fundamental aspects of social life, such as morality, ethics, and justice.

2. Effectiveness

- Folkways are less effective in shaping behavior, as violating them may result in mild social disapproval or ridicule.

- Mores are more effective, as violating them can lead to severe social disapproval, punishment, or even exclusion from the group.

3. Moral Guidance

- Folkways do not provide clear guidance on right and wrong, as they are more related to social conventions and customs.

- Mores help determine values of right and wrong, providing a moral framework for behavior that is considered essential for the well-being of society.

4. Changeability

- Folkways change relatively quickly, as they are less deep-rooted in society and can be influenced by changing social contexts, cultural exchange, or technological advancements.

- Mores are more resistant to change, as they are deeply ingrained in societal values and norms, and changes to them can have significant social implications.

5. Impact of Occupational Change

- Occupational changes can influence folkways, as individuals adapt to new social contexts, norms, and expectations.

- Mores, however, remain relatively stable despite occupational changes, reflecting deeper societal values and norms that transcend specific occupations or roles. Implications of the Distinction

Understanding the distinctions between folkways and mores provides insight into the complex dynamics of social norms and their role in shaping individual behavior and societal values. Recognizing these differences can help us:

- Appreciate the significance of mores in maintaining social order and promoting collective well-being

- Understand the role of folkways in shaping everyday behavior and social interactions

- Navigate the complexities of social norms and expectations in different contexts

- Develop a more nuanced understanding of the relationship between social norms and individual behavior

By recognizing the distinctions between folkways and mores, we can gain a deeper understanding of the social norms that shape our behavior and interactions, and work towards creating a more harmonious and cohesive society.

V
Association

An association is a group of people organized for a specific purpose or limited number of purposes. It is a collective entity that comes together to achieve a common goal or set of goals.

Definitions of Association

Different sociologists have defined association in various ways:

- MacIver: A deliberately formed organization for collective pursuit of shared interests.

- Ginsberg: A group of social beings related by a common organization to secure specific ends.

- G.D.H. Cole: A group of persons pursuing a common purpose through cooperative action.

- Bogardus: A working together of people to achieve a shared purpose.

Key Features of Association

Associations have certain key features:

1. Common Purpose: Associations are formed to achieve a specific goal or set of goals.

2. Organized Structure: Associations have a deliberate organization and structure.

3. Collective Action: Members work together to achieve their shared objectives.

4. Shared Interests: Associations are based on shared interests or values among members.

Importance of Associations

Associations play a significant role in society, enabling individuals to come together and work towards common goals. They provide a platform for collective action, decision-making, and problem-solving.

By understanding associations, we can appreciate the power of collective action and the importance of organized efforts in achieving shared objectives. Associations can be found in various forms, including professional, social, cultural, and community organizations.

Essential Elements of an Association

To constitute an association, the following essential elements must be present:

1. Group of People: An association consists of a group of individuals who come together to form a collective entity.

2. Organized Structure: The group must have a certain level of organization, with rules and norms governing their behavior and interactions.

3. Common Purpose: The members of the association must share a common purpose or goal, which is specific in nature and guides their collective actions.

Examples of Associations

Various types of groups can be considered associations, including:

- Family: A family unit can be seen as an association, with shared goals and values.

- Church: A religious organization can be considered an association, with a common purpose and organized structure.

- Trade Union: A labor union is an association of workers who come together to pursue common interests and goals.

- Music Club: A group of people who share a passion for music and come together to pursue their interest can be considered an association.

By understanding the essential elements of an association, we can identify and appreciate the various forms that associations can take in different contexts.

Formation of Associations

Associations can be formed on various bases, including:

1. Duration

Associations can be categorized based on their duration into:

- Temporary Association: Formed for a short-term purpose, such as a flood relief association.

- Permanent Association: Established for long-term purposes, such as a state or a professional organization.

Other Bases of Formation

Associations can also be formed based on other criteria, such as:

- Interest: Shared interests or hobbies, such as a music club or sports team.

- Occupation: Professional associations, such as trade unions or medical associations.

- Community: Community-based associations, such as neighborhood organizations or cultural groups.

Understanding the different bases of association formation can help us appreciate the diversity of associations and their roles in society.

Formation of Associations Based on Power

Associations can be categorized based on the level of power and authority they possess. This classification is significant in understanding the role and influence of different associations in society.

1. Sovereign Association

- A sovereign association has supreme power and authority, often with the ability to make laws and enforce them.

- Example: State or government, which has the highest authority in a country and can exercise control over its citizens and territory.

2. Semi-Sovereign Association

- A semi-sovereign association possesses some level of autonomy and decision-making power, but its authority is limited by a higher power or authority.

- Example: University, which may have autonomy in academic matters but is still subject to government regulations and oversight.

3. Non-Sovereign Association

- A non-sovereign association has limited power and authority, often with no legal or coercive power over its members.

- Example: Clubs, social organizations, or voluntary associations, which rely on the voluntary participation and cooperation of their members.

Implications of Power Classification

Understanding the power dynamics of associations is essential in recognizing their potential impact on society and individuals. This classification can help us:

- Appreciate the role of sovereign associations in shaping public policy and governance

- Recognize the autonomy and decision-making capacity of semi-sovereign associations

- Understand the limitations and opportunities of non-sovereign associations in promoting social change and community engagement

By acknowledging the different levels of power and authority among associations, we can better navigate the complex social landscape and identify opportunities for collaboration and collective action.

Formation of Associations Based on Function

Associations can be categorized based on their primary function or purpose. This classification highlights the diverse roles that associations play in society.

1. Biological Function

- Associations formed to fulfill biological needs, such as:

- Family: provides a fundamental social unit for nurturing and supporting its members.

- Kinship ties: extend beyond immediate family to include relatives and clan members.

2. Vocational Function

- Associations formed to promote professional or occupational interests, such as:

- Teachers' association: aims to advance the interests of educators and improve education.

- Trade unions: represent workers' interests and negotiate with employers.

- Professional associations: promote expertise, set standards, and provide networking opportunities.

3. Recreation Function

- Associations formed for leisure, entertainment, or recreational purposes, such as:

- Sports clubs (e.g., tennis club, football club): provide a space for members to engage in sports and socialize.

- Hobby clubs (e.g., photography club, book club): allow members to pursue shared interests.

- Social clubs: offer opportunities for socializing, networking, and community building.

Other Functions

Associations can also serve other functions, such as:

- Social welfare: providing support and services to vulnerable populations.

- Cultural preservation: promoting and preserving cultural heritage, traditions, and values.

- Advocacy or activism: promoting social change, raising awareness, and influencing policy.

- Education or training: providing opportunities for skill development, knowledge sharing, and personal growth.

Significance of Functional Classification

Understanding the various functions of associations can help us:

- Appreciate the diverse contributions of associations to society.

- Identify the specific needs and interests that associations fulfill.

- Recognize the potential for collaboration and partnership between associations with different functions.

By acknowledging the different functions of associations, we can better understand their roles in shaping society and promoting individual well-being.

Characteristics of an Association

Associations have distinct characteristics that define their nature and purpose. Understanding these characteristics is essential to appreciating the role of associations in society.

1. Based on a Particular Set of Law

- Associations are formed and governed by a specific set of laws, rules, and regulations.

- Members are expected to adhere to these rules and regulations, which provide a framework for the association's operations.

2. Formed to Complete Specific Work

- Associations are established to achieve specific goals or objectives.

- Members work together to accomplish these goals, which can range from promoting professional interests to advocating for social change.

3. Human Group

- Associations are created by human beings for specific purposes.

- Members are individuals who share common interests, values, or goals.

4. Common Interest or Aim

- Associations are formed by individuals who share a common purpose or goal.

- Members are united by their shared interests or objectives, which can be social, economic, cultural, or political in nature.

5. Organisation

- Associations are organized groups of individuals working together to achieve specific goals.

- Examples include trade unions, professional associations, advocacy groups, and community organizations.

6. Cooperative Spirit

- Associations rely on the cooperative spirit of their members to achieve common purposes.

- Members work together, sharing resources, expertise, and knowledge, to accomplish their goals and promote their shared interests.

Implications of Association Characteristics

Understanding the characteristics of associations can help us:

- Appreciate the diversity of associations and their roles in society.

- Recognize the importance of cooperation and collective action in achieving shared goals.

- Identify opportunities for collaboration and partnership between associations.

- Analyze the impact of associations on individuals, communities, and society as a whole.

By acknowledging the characteristics of associations, we can better understand their significance and potential in shaping society and promoting individual well-being.

Difference between Institution and Association

Institutions and associations are both social structures that play important roles in shaping our lives and interactions. However, they have distinct differences in terms of their purpose, structure, and function.

1. Obligation to Obey Laws

- Institutions: Individuals are required to obey the laws and norms of an institution, which are often enforced by authority or tradition. For example, laws and norms governing family relationships or educational institutions.

- Associations: Individuals are required to obey the rules and regulations of an association only as long as they retain its membership. Members can choose to leave the association if they disagree with its rules or goals.

2. Evolutionary Character

- Institutions: Institutions evolve over time, shaped by historical, cultural, and social factors. They often have a long history and are deeply ingrained in society. Examples include family, education, and government.

- Associations: Associations can be created at any time, with a specific purpose or goal. They may be more flexible and adaptable to changing circumstances.

3. Basis of Laws

- Institutions: The laws and norms of institutions are often based on tradition, custom, or dogma. They may be influenced by cultural, religious, or historical factors.

- Associations: The rules and regulations of associations are often based on rational deliberations and agreements among its founder members. They may be more flexible and open to revision.

4. Permanence

- Institutions: Institutions tend to be more permanent, with a long history and established practices. They often play a critical role in shaping society and culture.

- Associations: Associations may be more temporary or flexible, with a specific purpose or goal that can be achieved over time. They may dissolve or change as circumstances change.

5. Purpose and Function

- Institutions: Institutions meet basic needs and objectives of social life, such as family, education, or government. They provide a framework for social interaction and cooperation.

- Associations: Associations meet secondary needs and interests of individuals, such as hobbies, professional development, or socializing. They provide opportunities for individuals to pursue shared interests and goals.

6. Indication

- Institutions: Institutions indicate a specific purpose or function, such as marriage, education, or government. They often have a clear role and responsibility in society.

- Associations: Associations indicate the number of persons associated with it, such as a club, organization, or group. They may have a more flexible or variable structure.

7. Structure

- Institutions: Institutions have a definite structure, shaped by tradition, custom, or law. They often have a hierarchical or formal organization.

- Associations: Associations may have a flexible or variable structure, depending on its purpose and goals. They may be more informal or decentralized.

8. Nature

- Institutions: Institutions are formless and abstract, representing a set of norms, values, and practices. They often have a profound impact on society and culture.

- Associations: Associations have a concrete form, with a physical presence, membership, and activities. They are often more tangible and visible than institutions.

9. Social Condition

- Institutions: Institutions represent a social condition of conduct and behavior based on rules of procedure. They often shape social norms and expectations.

- Associations: Associations represent a collective effort to achieve a specific goal or purpose. They often provide opportunities for social interaction, cooperation, and mutual support.

Understanding the differences between institutions and associations can help us appreciate the complex social structures that shape our lives and interactions. By recognizing the distinct characteristics of each, we can better navigate the social landscape and identify opportunities for cooperation and collective action.

Difference between Institution and Society

Institutions and society are interconnected but distinct concepts. Understanding their differences is essential to appreciating the complex social structures that shape our lives.

1. Definition

- Society: A system of social relationships among individuals, groups, and institutions. It encompasses the complex web of interactions, norms, and values that shape human behavior. Society is a broad concept that refers to the collective whole of people, their relationships, and their institutions.

- Institution: An organization of rules, traditions, and usages that govern social behavior. Institutions provide a framework for social interaction, stability, and order. Examples of institutions include family, education, government, and economy.

2. Relationship with Society

- Institutions: Are recognized and accepted by society, providing a framework for social interaction and behavior. Institutions are part of the social fabric, shaping individual and collective behavior. They help to regulate social behavior, resolve conflicts, and promote cooperation.

- Society: Provides the context and framework for institutions to operate. Society influences the development, functioning, and evolution of institutions. Institutions are shaped by the values, norms, and interests of the society in which they operate.

3. Purpose and Function

- Institutions: Exist to govern relationships between members of society, providing stability and order. Institutions help to:
- Regulate social behavior
- Resolve conflicts
- Promote cooperation
- Provide stability and predictability

- Society: Represents the collective interests and needs of its members. Society provides a framework for social interaction, cooperation, and mutual support. Society is concerned with the well-being, needs, and interests of its members.

4. Focus

- Society: Represents the human aspect, focusing on social relationships and interactions. Society is concerned with the well-being, needs, and interests of its members. It encompasses the social, economic, and cultural aspects of human life.

- Institution: Represents a social condition of conduct and behavior, focusing on rules, norms, and expectations. Institutions provide a framework for social behavior, shaping individual and collective actions. Institutions are concerned with maintaining social order, stability, and predictability.

Key Distinctions

- Institutions are part of society: Institutions are embedded in society and play a crucial role in shaping social behavior and interactions.

- Society is a broader concept: Society encompasses multiple institutions, as well as informal social relationships and networks. Society is a complex system that includes institutions, culture, norms, and values.

- Institutions provide structure: Institutions provide a framework for social interaction, stability, and order, while society provides the context and framework for institutions to operate.

Implications

Understanding the differences between institutions and society can help us:

- Appreciate the complex social dynamics that shape our lives and interactions.

- Recognize the role of institutions in shaping social behavior and promoting stability and order.

- Identify opportunities for social change and reform, and develop strategies to promote positive social outcomes.

- Analyze the relationships between institutions and society, and understand how they influence each other.

By acknowledging the distinctions between institutions and society, we can better understand the complex social structures that shape our lives and interactions. This understanding can help us navigate the social world, make informed decisions, and contribute to the development of a more just and equitable society.

VI
Kinship

Kinship refers to the complex system of relationships based on blood ties, marriage, and adoption. According to Charles Winick, kinship systems include socially recognized relationships based on both actual and supposed genealogical ties. Dr. D.N. Mazumdar further emphasizes that kinship is a universal and fundamental bond that ties people together, based on reproduction and including relationships by blood (consanguineous), marriage (affinal), and kindred ones such as adopted children. Kinship is a fundamental aspect of human society, and its importance varies across different cultures and social contexts. In primitive societies, kinship plays a crucial role in assigning economic and political functions, acquiring rights and obligations, and receiving community aid. Even in modern societies, kinship remains important in controlling individual behavior and providing mutual aid, particularly in industrial working-class communities and upper-class families.

Kinship can be categorized into different types, including consanguineous kinship based on blood relationships, affinal kinship based on marriage, and kindred kinship based on adoption or other forms of kinship ties. The significance of kinship extends beyond individual relationships, influencing social structures and institutions. While its impact on modern societies may be limited, kinship continues to shape social behavior, cultural norms, and individual identities.

Types of Kinship

Kinship can be classified into two main types:

- Affinal Kinship: Based on the bond of marriage, affinal kinship creates a host of relationships, such as brother-in-law, son-in-law, daughter-in-law, and more. These relationships are formed through marriage and are an essential part of social networks.

- Consanguineous Kinship: Based on the bond of blood, consanguineous kinship includes relationships between parents and children, siblings, and other relatives related through blood. This type of kinship is fundamental to understanding family structures and social relationships.

Degree of Kinship

Relatives can be classified into different categories based on their nearness or distance:

- Primary Kin: Close and direct relatives, such as:
- Husband-wife
- Father-son
- Mother-daughter
- Father-daughter
- Mother-son
- Younger-elder brothers
- Younger-elder sisters
- Sister-brother

These relationships are typically characterized by strong emotional bonds and frequent interaction.

- Secondary Kin: Primary kin of primary kin, such as:
- Father's brother (chacha)
- Sister's husband (bahnoi)
- Mother's sister (masi)
- Father's sister (bua)

These relationships are important for building social networks and providing support.

- Tertiary Kin: Secondary kin of primary kin or primary kin of secondary kin, such as:
  - Wife of brother-in-law (sahraj)
  - Brother-in-law of brother
  - Husband of mother's sister (mama)

These relationships can be significant in certain social contexts, such as in extended family structures.

Significance of Kinship

Kinship plays a vital role in shaping social relationships, cultural norms, and individual identities. Understanding kinship is essential for:

- Navigating complex relationships: Kinship helps individuals understand their roles and responsibilities within their social networks.
- Building social support: Kinship relationships can provide emotional, financial, and practical support.
- Understanding cultural norms: Kinship is often tied to cultural norms and expectations, influencing behavior and decision-making.
- Shaping individual identities: Kinship can influence an individual's sense of belonging, identity, and self-concept.

According to Murdock, there are 33 secondary and 151 tertiary kin of a person. Understanding the degree of kinship helps in navigating complex relationships and social structures.

Kinship Terms

Kinship terms are words used to describe relationships between individuals in a family or social network. These terms help to identify and classify different types of kin.

Classification of Kinship Terms

Morgan's study of kinship terms identified two main systems:

- Classificatory System: This system uses a single term to refer to multiple kin relationships. Examples include:
  - Uncle (referring to chacha, mama, mausa, foofa, etc.)
  - Nephew
  - Cousin

- Samadhin (referring to parents of daughter-in-law and son-in-law)
- Bua (father's sister) and mausi (mother's sister) being referred to by a single term in some cultures
- Descriptive System: This system uses specific terms to describe exact relationships. Examples include:
- Father
- Mother
- Chacha (father's younger brother)
- Mausaji (mother's brother)
- Sala (wife's brother)
- Bahnoi (sister's husband)
- Bhabhi (brother's wife)
- Devar (husband's younger brother)

Characteristics of Kinship Terms

- Mixed usage: Both classificatory and descriptive systems are used in most societies, and it's rare to find a pure form of either system.
- Cultural significance: Kinship terms reflect cultural norms, values, and social relationships.
- Contextual importance: Understanding kinship terms is essential for navigating complex social relationships and communicating effectively within families and communities.
- Variability: Kinship terms can vary across cultures, languages, and regions, highlighting the diversity of human social relationships.

Importance of Kinship Terms

- Social organization: Kinship terms help to organize social relationships and define roles and responsibilities.
- Communication: Kinship terms facilitate communication and clarify relationships within families and communities.
- Cultural identity: Kinship terms are an integral part of cultural identity and can influence an individual's sense of belonging and self-concept.

By understanding kinship terms, we can gain insights into the complex web of social relationships that shape human societies.

Functions of Kinship

Kinship serves several important purposes in societies:

- Transmission of status and property: Kinship provides a way of transmitting status, property, and social position from one generation to the next.

- Establishing and maintaining social groups: In some societies, kinship helps to establish and maintain effective social groups, fostering cooperation and mutual support.

Key Functions of Kinship

- Economic cooperation: Kins often help with economic tasks or other activities that require cooperation, such as farming, business, or household chores.

- Social support: Kins are expected to provide support and assistance in times of need, such as during ceremonies, crises, or other significant events.

- Social solidarity: Kinship helps to maintain solidarity within families and communities, promoting a sense of belonging and shared identity.

- Cultural transmission: Kinship plays a role in transmitting cultural values, norms, and practices from one generation to the next.

Importance of Kinship in Social Life

- Marriage ceremonies: Kins are often invited to marriage ceremonies and other significant events, highlighting the importance of kinship ties.

- Religious activities: Kins may participate in religious activities and ceremonies, demonstrating the role of kinship in shaping cultural and spiritual practices.

- Crisis support: Kins are often relied upon for aid and support during times of crisis, such as financial difficulties or personal emergencies.

- Socialization: Kinship plays a role in socializing individuals, teaching them cultural norms, values, and expectations.

Challenges in Kinship Relationships

- Tensions and conflicts: Kinship relationships can be strained due to factors like discriminatory rights, property disputes, or conflicting interests.

- Property disputes: In propertied classes, kinship relationships can be complicated by disputes over inheritance, property rights, or other economic interests.

- Changing social norms: Changes in social norms and values can lead to tensions and conflicts within kinship relationships.

Significance of Kinship

- Shaping social relationships: Kinship plays a crucial role in shaping social relationships, cultural practices, and individual identities.

- Providing support: Kinship provides a safety net for individuals, offering support and assistance in times of need.

- Cultural continuity: Kinship helps to maintain cultural continuity, transmitting values, norms, and practices from one generation to the next.

Overall, kinship is a vital aspect of human social organization, influencing various aspects of life, from economic cooperation to cultural transmission.

Kinship Usages

Kinship usages refer to the behavior patterns and social norms that govern relationships between different kin. These usages regulate interactions, define roles, and provide guidelines for acceptable behavior.

Types of Kinship Usages

- Avoidance: A usage where two kin are expected to avoid each other, often due to social or cultural norms. Examples include:
- Father-in-law and daughter-in-law
- Son-in-law and mother-in-law
- Pardah system in Hindu families
- Joking relationship: A usage where two kin are permitted to tease or make fun of each other. Examples include:
- Devar (husband's younger brother) and bhabhi (brother's wife)

- Jija (sister's husband) and sali (wife's sister)
- Teknonymy: A usage where a kin is referred to indirectly through another kin. Example:
- A wife referring to her husband as the father of her child
- Avunclate: A usage where the maternal uncle (mama) has a special role and obligations towards his nephews and nieces.
- Amitate: A usage where the father's sister is given a special role and respect.
- Couvade: A usage where the husband mimics the behavior of his wife during childbirth, often observing taboos and restrictions.

Functions of Kinship Usages

- Creating groups: Kinship usages help create special groupings of kin, such as families.
- Governing role relationships: Kinship usages provide guidelines for interactions between kin, defining proper and acceptable behavior.
- Regularizing social life: Kinship usages help regulate social life, providing a framework for behavior and interaction.
- Reducing conflict: Kinship usages can help reduce conflict by providing clear guidelines for behavior and interaction.

Significance of Kinship Usages

- Cultural significance: Kinship usages reflect cultural norms and values, shaping social relationships and behavior.
- Social organization: Kinship usages play a crucial role in organizing social life, defining roles and responsibilities.
- Individual behavior: Kinship usages can influence individual behavior, providing guidelines for interaction and relationship-building.
- Social cohesion: Kinship usages can promote social cohesion by providing a shared understanding of behavior and interaction.

Variations in Kinship Usages

- Cultural variation: Kinship usages can vary significantly across cultures, reflecting different social norms and values.
- Contextual influence: Kinship usages can be influenced by contextual factors, such as social change or modernization.

- Individual differences: Kinship usages can be shaped by individual differences, such as personality or life experiences.

Importance of Studying Kinship Usages

- Understanding social relationships: Studying kinship usages can provide insights into social relationships and behavior.

- Cultural understanding: Kinship usages can provide a window into cultural norms and values.

- Social policy: Understanding kinship usages can inform social policy, particularly in areas such as family law or social welfare.

Overall, kinship usages are essential in shaping social relationships, cultural practices, and individual identities.

VII

Marriage

Marriage and family are fundamental social institutions that shape the lives of individuals and societies. These institutions are built on a complex web of social norms, values, and relationships that govern human behavior.

Marriage as a Social Institution

Marriage is a socially recognized union between two individuals that provides a foundation for family formation and child-rearing. It is a complex institution that involves not only the couple but also their families, communities, and society at large. Marriage is often characterized by certain rights and duties, such as emotional support, financial cooperation, and shared responsibilities.

Family as a Social Institution

Family is a fundamental social institution that provides a nurturing environment for individuals, particularly children. It is a complex web of relationships that involves not only biological ties but also social and emotional bonds. Family structures and dynamics can vary significantly across cultures and societies, reflecting different social norms and values.

Importance of Marriage and Family

Marriage and family are essential institutions that provide numerous benefits for individuals and societies. Some of the key importance of marriage and family include:

- Emotional support: Marriage and family provide emotional support and a sense of belonging for individuals.

- Socialization: Family plays a crucial role in socializing individuals, teaching them social norms, values, and behaviors.

- Economic cooperation: Marriage and family often involve economic cooperation, providing a foundation for financial stability and security.

- Child-rearing: Family provides a nurturing environment for children, shaping their physical, emotional, and cognitive development.

Challenges Facing Marriage and Family

Marriage and family are facing numerous challenges in modern societies, including:

- Changing social norms: Changing social norms and values are redefining traditional notions of marriage and family.

- Increased divorce rates: Rising divorce rates are changing the dynamics of family structures and relationships.

- Single-parent households: Single-parent households are becoming increasingly common, presenting unique challenges for individuals and societies.

- Globalization and migration: Globalization and migration are creating new challenges for marriage and family, particularly in terms of cultural adaptation and integration.

Conclusion

Marriage and family are fundamental social institutions that shape the lives of individuals and societies. These institutions provide numerous benefits, including emotional support, socialization, economic cooperation, and child-rearing. However, marriage and family are also facing numerous challenges in modern societies, including changing social norms, increased divorce rates, single-parent households, and globalization and migration. Understanding the complexities of marriage and family is essential for building strong, resilient relationships and communities.

Definitions of Marriage

Marriage has been defined in various ways by different sociologists and anthropologists. Some of the key definitions include:

- Jacob and Stern: "Marriage is a term for social relationship of husband and wife or of plural mates, also used for the ceremony of uniting marital partners."

- Ernest R. Groves: "Marriage is a public confession and legal registration of an adventure in fellowship."

- Lundberg: Marriage consists "The rules and regulations which define the rights, duties and privileges of husband and wife, with respect to each other."

- Hoebel: "Marriage is the complex of social norms that define and control the relations of mated pairs, to each other, their kinsmen, their offspring and society."

- Lowee: "Marriage denotes those unequivocally sanctioned unions which persist beyond sensuous satisfaction and thus come to underline family life."

Key Elements of Marriage

Based on the definitions, some of the key elements of marriage include:

- Union between individuals: Marriage involves a union between one or more men and one or more women.

- Social sanction: Marriage requires social sanction, often in the form of a ceremony or ritual.

- Rights and responsibilities: Marriage involves certain rights and responsibilities between the partners and towards their children.

- Biological and sociological functions: Marriage serves both biological functions (mating) and sociological functions (care of children, maintenance of household).

Importance of Social Sanction

Social sanction is a crucial aspect of marriage, as it:

- Authorizes relationships: Social sanction authorizes the relationship between the partners, allowing them to engage in sexual and other social and economic relations.

- Defines roles and responsibilities: Social sanction helps define the roles and responsibilities of the partners and their families.

- Provides legitimacy: Social sanction provides legitimacy to the marriage and the children born within it.

Variations in Marriage

Marriage can take different forms and have different characteristics, including:

- Different forms of marriage: Marriage can be monogamous or polygamous, and can involve different types of relationships.

- Cultural variations: Marriage customs and practices can vary significantly across cultures.

- Social and economic factors: Marriage can be influenced by social and economic factors, such as family background, education, and economic status.

Forms of Marriage

There are several forms of marriage, each with its unique characteristics and cultural significance.

- Monogamy: A form of marriage where one man marries one woman.

- Polygamy: A form of marriage where one individual marries multiple partners. Polygamy can be further divided into:

- Polygyny: A form of marriage where one man marries multiple women.

- Polyandry: A form of marriage where one woman marries multiple men.

- Group Marriage: A hypothetical form of marriage where all brothers of a family marry all sisters of another family.

Polyandry

Polyandry is a form of marriage where one woman marries multiple men at the same time. It's a relatively rare form of marriage, but it's practiced in some societies.

- Types of Polyandry: There are two main types of polyandry:

- Fraternal Polyandry: One wife is shared among brothers, and the children are treated as the offspring of the eldest brother.

- Non-fraternal Polyandry: One woman has multiple husbands who are not necessarily brothers.

- Societies Practicing Polyandry: Polyandry is practiced in various societies, including Tibet, the Todas of Malabar, and some tribes in Africa and South America.

Characteristics of Polyandry

Polyandry has several characteristics that distinguish it from other forms of marriage:

- Shared Responsibilities: In polyandrous societies, the husbands often share responsibilities, such as childcare and economic support.

- Complex Family Structure: Polyandry can lead to complex family structures, where multiple men are involved in raising children.

- Cultural Significance: Polyandry is often tied to cultural practices and traditions, reflecting the values and norms of a society.

Advantages and Disadvantages of Polyandry

Polyandry has both advantages and disadvantages:

- Advantages: Polyandry can provide economic benefits, such as shared resources and labor. It can also help to ensure that property remains within the family.

- Disadvantages: Polyandry can lead to conflicts and jealousy among the husbands. It can also create complex family dynamics and relationships.

Conclusion

Polyandry is a unique form of marriage that is practiced in some societies. It has its own characteristics, advantages, and disadvantages. Understanding polyandry can provide insights into the diversity of human relationships and cultural practices.

VIII
Family

Family institution is a fundamental and enduring aspect of human society, serving as both an institution and an association. As the oldest institution, family has been a cornerstone of social structure, providing a foundation for social organization and stability. It is a primary group where individuals first experience social interaction and relationships, and its universality is evident across cultures and societies. Family plays a crucial role in socializing individuals, teaching them social norms, values, and behaviors, while also providing emotional support and economic security. The institution of family is shaped by various factors, including the sexual urge, socio-economic expediency, and cultural traditions. Through its role in passing on cultural values and practices to future generations, family helps to preserve societal heritage and promote continuity. As a vital component of human society, family remains an essential part of individual and collective well-being, influencing personal development, social relationships, and community cohesion.

Here's the information about the meaning and definitions of family:

Meaning of Family

The term "family" has evolved from the Roman word "famulus" and Latin word "familia", which referred to a household or servants.

Today, family refers to a group of individuals related by blood, marriage, or adoption, living together or connected through kinship ties.

Definitions of Family

Various sociologists and researchers have defined family in different ways:

- Clare: "A system of relationships existing between parents and children."

- MacIver: "A group defined by a sex relationship sufficiently precise and enduring to provide for the procreation and up-bringing of children."

- Burgess and Locke: "A group of persons united by the ties of marriage, blood or adoption constituting a single household, interacting and inter-communicating with each other in their respective social role."

- Elliot and Merill: "The biological, social unit composed of husband, wife and children."

- Ogburn and Nimkoff: "Family is more or less durable association of husband and wife without children or of a man or woman alone."

- Murdock: "Family is a social group characterised by common residence, economic cooperation and reproduction."

Key Elements of Family

Based on the definitions, some key elements of family include:

- Kinship ties: Family is often defined by kinship ties, including blood relations, marriage, or adoption.

- Common residence: Family members often live together or share a common residence.

- Economic cooperation: Family members may cooperate economically, sharing resources and responsibilities.

- Social relationships: Family involves complex social relationships, including roles and responsibilities.

Importance of Family

Family plays a vital role in shaping individual and societal well-being, influencing:

- Socialization: Family socializes individuals, teaching them social norms, values, and behaviors.

- Emotional support: Family provides emotional support and a sense of belonging to its members.

- Economic security: Family can provide economic security and support to its members.

Conclusion

The concept of family is complex and multifaceted, encompassing various definitions and interpretations. Understanding the meaning and definitions of family can provide insights into the importance of family in shaping individual and societal well-being.

The origin of family is a complex and debated topic among scholars, with its roots tracing back to ancient times. It's challenging to determine whether family originated from marriage or vice versa. Evidence from archaeological finds at Harappa and Mohenjo-Daro, as well as references in ancient Tamil literature, suggest that family systems existed even before the Vedic age. The Vedic period emphasized the sacredness of marriage ties, highlighting the importance of family relationships and ideals. The family ideal of the Vedic people was very high, as reflected in their invocations and literature, such as the meaningful invocation, "Be, thou, mother of heroic children, devoted to the Gods. Be, thou, Queen in thy father-in-law's household. May all the Gods unite the hearts of us two into one." Despite the uncertainty surrounding its exact origin, family has been a vital part of human society, shaping social relationships, providing emotional support, and influencing cultural transmission.

Theories of the Origin of Family

There are several theories about the origin of family, each with its own strengths and limitations.

1. Theory of Sex Communism

This theory suggests that family originated from a state of unrestricted sexual relationships between men and women. However, this theory is not widely accepted by modern sociologists.

2. Patriarchal Theory

This theory proposes that family originated with the authority of the patriarch or male head of the household. While patriarchal families have existed in the past and present, this theory is not considered a sound explanation for the origin of family.

3. Matriarchal Theory

This theory suggests that family originated with the mother or female head of the household. Like the patriarchal theory, the matriarchal theory is not widely accepted as an explanation for the origin of family.

4. Monogamy Theory

This theory, propounded by Westermarck, suggests that family originated from monogamous relationships. According to this theory, the male's feeling of ownership and jealousy led to the formation of family. However, this theory has been criticized for not providing a complete explanation of the origin of family.

5. Multi-Factor Theory

Modern sociologists propose that the origin of family cannot be attributed to a single factor. Instead, they suggest that multiple factors contributed to the emergence of family, including biological, social, and cultural factors. This theory acknowledges the complexity of family origins and recognizes that different societies may have developed family structures in response to unique circumstances.

Reasons for the Origin of Family

Several factors are believed to have contributed to the origin of family:

1. Sexual needs: The satisfaction of sexual needs is considered a fundamental aspect of human nature, and family may have originated as a way to regulate and fulfill these needs.

2. Desire for permanent cooperation and offspring: The desire for permanent cooperation and the need for offspring to perpetuate the family line may have also contributed to the origin of family.

3. Economic needs: Economic cooperation and mutual support may have been another factor that led to the formation of family

units.

4. Desire for procreation and children: The desire for children and the need for procreation are fundamental human instincts that may have played a role in the origin of family.

5. Need for a life partner: The need for a partner to share life's joys and sorrows may have also contributed to the origin of family.

6. Fulfillment of life's aims: In some cultures, family life is seen as essential for fulfilling life's aims, such as the four purusharthas (Kama, Artha, Dharma, and Moksha).

Evolutionary Theory

The evolutionary theory, proposed by Morgan, suggests that family has passed through several stages:

- Five stages: Morgan identified five stages in the evolution of family, although the specific stages are not mentioned in the provided text.

- Complex evolution: The evolution of family is seen as a complex process, influenced by various factors, including biological, social, and cultural changes.

Sociological Perspectives

Sociologists such as Ralph Linton and MacIver have offered insights into the origin and evolution of family:

- Multiple lines of evolution: Linton suggests that societies have followed multiple lines of evolution, rather than a single consistent line.

- Complex of human desires: MacIver writes that family systems arise from a complex of human desires and conscious needs, finding different expressions in different environments.

Different Types of Families

Based on Residence

1. Matrilocal Residence. In it residence of female has got more importance than that of the male member. In fact, husband moves to the residence of wife and begins to live there.

matrilocal residence and in it wife lives in the residence of the husband. This is quite common these days th 3. Changing Residence. In this system neither husband nor wife permanently lives in each other's resideher but live alternatively at each other's resideh oth

4. Bilocal Residence Family. The married couple may choose between establishing their residence with the bridegroom's parents or with the bride's parents.

5. Avunculocal Residence Family. The bride and bridegroom go to live with the bridegroom's maternal uncle that is the brother of the bridegroom's mother. In a combination of matrilocal and avunculocal residence, the couple lives in alternative years with the bride's parents and the bridegroom's maternal uncle.

Types of Families Based on Authority

Families can be classified based on the distribution of authority and power within the household. Two primary types of families based on authority are:

1. Patriarchal Family

A patriarchal family is characterized by the concentration of authority and decision-making power in the hands of the male members, typically the father or the eldest male. In this type of family, men hold significant influence over family decisions, finances, and social interactions. Patriarchal families are often associated with traditional and conservative values, where men are seen as the primary breadwinners and decision-makers.

2. Matriarchal Family

A matriarchal family, on the other hand, is defined by the transmission of name, status, and material inheritance through the female line. In a matriarchal family:

- Descent is traced through the mother, and children often take their mother's surname.

- The family often resides at the home of the mother, and the husband may move to the wife's residence after marriage.

- The husband may have a secondary position in the home, with the wife's brothers holding more authority and influence.

- Authority in the family may belong to a male representative of the wife's kin, such as her brother or maternal uncle.

Characteristics of Matriarchal Families

Matriarchal families have distinct features, including:

- Kinship ties are often stronger than conjugal bonds, with a greater emphasis on relationships between siblings and other relatives.

- The maternal system tends to unite the kin-group but may weaken the conjugal family, as the primary focus is on the family of origin rather than the nuclear family.

- Matriarchal families are often associated with the principle of exogamy, where the tribe is divided into separate intermarrying groups.

Prevalence of Matriarchal Families

While it is uncertain whether matriarchal families were prevalent in all primitive societies, matriarchal family systems still exist in many parts of the world today. Examples of matriarchal societies can be found in certain indigenous cultures, such as the Minangkabau people of Indonesia and the Mosuo people of China.

Implications of Matriarchal Families

Matriarchal families offer valuable insights into alternative forms of family organization and authority structures. They challenge traditional patriarchal norms and highlight the importance of female empowerment and decision-making. Understanding matriarchal families can also inform policies and programs aimed at promoting gender equality and supporting diverse family forms.

Conclusion

In conclusion, families based on authority can be classified into patriarchal and matriarchal types, each with distinct characteristics and implications. While patriarchal families are more common in many societies, matriarchal families offer a unique perspective on family dynamics and authority structures. By recognizing and appreciating the diversity of family forms, we can work towards creating more inclusive and supportive environments for all families.

Key Features of Matriarchal Families

The following are key features of matriarchal families:

a) Descent Traced Through Mother

In matriarchal families, descent is traced through the mother, meaning that children take their mother's surname and inherit property and social status from her. This emphasizes the importance of maternal lineage and the role of women in passing down family traditions and assets.

b) Residence at Mother's Home

In most cases, the family resides at the home of the mother. The husband often has a secondary position in the home and may be regarded as having a lower status than the brothers of his wife. This arrangement reflects the matrilocal residence pattern, where the wife's family plays a central role in family life.

c) Authority Belongs to Male Representative of Wife's Kin

Due to the matrilineal system, authority in the family frequently belongs to a male representative of the wife's kin, such as her brother or maternal uncle. This means that men play an important role in decision-making, but their authority is derived from their relationship to the wife's family rather than their own family. This unique distribution of power highlights the complex dynamics of matriarchal families.

d) Impact on Kin-Group and Conjugal Family

According to MacIver and Page, the maternal system tends to:

- Unite the kin-group (or "consanguine family") together, emphasizing the importance of blood relationships and family ties.

- Lessen the cohesiveness of the 'conjugal' family itself, potentially leading to a weaker bond between spouses. This can result in a greater emphasis on relationships between siblings and other relatives.

- Be associated with the principle of exogamy, where the tribe is divided into separate intermarrying groups. This practice can help to promote social cohesion and prevent conflicts within the community.

Implications of Matriarchal Family Structure

The matriarchal family structure has several implications for family dynamics and social organization:

- Women play a central role in family decision-making and inheritance.

- Men have important roles, but their authority is often derived from their relationship to the wife's family.

- Family ties and kinship relationships are emphasized over conjugal relationships.

- The matrilineal system can promote social cohesion and cooperation within the community.

By understanding the key features and implications of matriarchal families, we can gain a deeper appreciation for the diversity of family structures and social organizations across cultures.

Essential Functions of Family in Modern Society

Despite many functions of family being taken over by other associations, family continues to perform some essential functions that are vital for the well-being and development of its members. Some of these essential functions include:

1. Satisfaction of Sex Needs

Satisfaction of sex and instincts is one of the essential functions of a family. Marriage and family provide a socially accepted outlet for sexual needs, promoting emotional and physical well-being. A healthy and fulfilling relationship between partners is essential for a stable family environment.

2. Reproduction of Children

Reproduction is the primary aim of family, and it includes not only giving birth to children but also looking after them and bringing them up well. Family provides a nurturing environment for children to grow and develop, and parents play a crucial role in shaping their children's physical, emotional, and social development.

3. Providing for Minimum Basic Facilities

It is the responsibility of the head of the family to provide some minimum basic facilities to the members of the family, including food, clothing, and shelter. Other members of the family also contribute to maintaining a comfortable and secure living environment. This function ensures that family members have their basic needs met, allowing them to focus on personal growth and development.

4. Giving Love and Sympathy

Family members are supposed to solve each other's problems with a sympathetic and careful attitude. Children require affection from their parents, and spouses need love and support from each other. Emotional support and love are essential for building strong family bonds, promoting emotional well-being, and fostering a sense of belonging.

5. Socialisation of Members

Family is the first socialising institution, where children learn important values, norms, and habits. The Indian system of graduated sanskaras is a regulated process of socialization that helps internalize norms and values. Family plays a crucial role in shaping the social and cultural identity of its members, influencing their worldview, and preparing them for their roles in society.

6. Protection of the Young

The most essential function of the family is to protect the young carefully. Children are vulnerable and depend on their family for safety, security, and protection. Family provides a nurturing environment that allows children to grow and develop without undue risk or danger, ensuring their physical, emotional, and psychological well-being.

Importance of Family Functions

The essential functions of family are vital for the well-being and development of its members. By performing these functions, family provides a supportive and nurturing environment that allows individuals to grow, develop, and thrive. Family functions also play a crucial role in shaping individual and societal values, norms, and behaviors.

Challenges to Family Functions

Despite the importance of family functions, families face various challenges in modern society. These challenges include:

- Changing family structures and dynamics
- Increased mobility and migration
- Economic pressures and financial stress
- Social and cultural changes
- Impact of technology on family relationships

Conclusion

In conclusion, family continues to play a vital role in modern society, performing essential functions that promote the physical, emotional, and social well-being of its members. By understanding these functions and the challenges families face, we can work towards supporting and strengthening families, ultimately contributing to the well-being of individuals and society as a whole.

Non-Essential Functions of Family

While essential functions of family are vital for the survival and well-being of its members, non-essential functions play a significant role in shaping the social, cultural, and economic aspects of family life. Some of the non-essential functions of family include:

1. Economic Functions

The family is responsible for the proper distribution of work according to the capacity of each member. Family members work together to meet their economic needs, and the family ensures that each member gets the necessary resources to meet their needs. Family also looks after family property and manages its economic resources.

2. Social Functions

Family determines an individual's social status and earning capacity. Family exercises social control over its members, ensuring they obey moral norms and do not engage in anti-social activities. Family also preserves customs and conventions, passing them down from one generation to the next.

3. Religious Functions

Family provides religious training to children, teaching them various religious virtues. Family members participate in religious practices, such as worship, rituals, and ceremonies, which shape their spiritual identity.

4. Educational Functions

Family is the first school for a child, where they learn through imitation and observation. Family provides general education and arranges for vocational education, helping members acquire skills and knowledge.

5. Health Functions

Family takes care of the health of its members, ensuring they receive proper medical attention when needed. Family members support each other during illness, providing emotional and physical care.

6. Recreational Functions

Family observes recreational functions, such as celebrating festivals, singing, and dancing together. Family members also visit relatives and friends, promoting social bonding and relaxation.

7. Cultural Functions

Family preserves its cultural heritage, passing down customs, codes, and traditions to the next generation. Family environment shapes a child's personality, influencing their worldview and cultural identity.

8. Formation of Personality Traits

Family plays a significant role in shaping an individual's personality traits, influencing their sentiments, values, and behavior. Family tradition and customs shape a child's basic personality traits, which are handed down from generation to generation.

Importance of Non-Essential Functions

Non-essential functions of family are important because they:
- Shape individual and family identity
- Influence social and cultural norms
- Promote emotional and social well-being
- Provide a sense of belonging and connection

- Support personal growth and development

Impact on Family Dynamics

Non-essential functions of family can have a significant impact on family dynamics, including:

- Strengthening family bonds and relationships
- Promoting cultural and social continuity
- Shaping individual values and behavior
- Influencing family decision-making and problem-solving
- Enhancing family cohesion and solidarity

Challenges to Non-Essential Functions

Non-essential functions of family can be challenged by various factors, including:

- Changing social and cultural norms
- Economic pressures and financial stress
- Increased mobility and migration
- Impact of technology on family relationships
- Shifting family values and priorities

Conclusion

In conclusion, non-essential functions of family play a vital role in shaping the social, cultural, and economic aspects of family life. By understanding these functions and their importance, we can appreciate the complexity and richness of family relationships and dynamics.

IX
Economic Institution

Economic institutions refer to the social structures and systems that govern the production, distribution, and consumption of goods and services within a society. These institutions play a crucial role in shaping the economic behavior of individuals and groups, and they help to allocate scarce resources in a way that meets the needs and wants of society.

According to Kingsley Davis, economic institutions are those basic ideas, norms, and statutes that govern the allocation of scarce goods in any society. Ogburn and Nimkoff define economic institutions as the activities of men in relation to food and property, which constitute the economic institutions. Dressler views economic institutions as the cultural system of society directly concerned with the production, distribution, and consumption of goods and services.

The main function of economic institutions is to provide the means by which the members of a society may survive and maintain themselves. Economic institutions are involved in various economic activities, including production, distribution, and consumption. They govern the way in which goods and services are produced, allocated, and used within a society.

Economic institutions are essential to the functioning of society, as they provide the framework for economic activity and help to allocate scarce resources in a way that meets the needs and wants of individuals and groups. By understanding economic institutions, we can gain valuable insights into the workings of the economy and the ways in which society shapes economic behavior.

Preliminary Concepts in Economics

Utility

Utility is a fundamental concept in economics that refers to the capacity of goods or services to satisfy human needs and wants. It is the ability of a product or service to provide satisfaction or pleasure to consumers. Utility can be derived from various sources, including tangible goods, intangible services, and experiences. The concept of utility is subjective, meaning that it varies from person to person and depends on individual preferences and tastes.

Wealth

Wealth refers to the accumulation of valuable economic goods or services that an individual or organization possesses. Wealth can take many forms, including financial assets, physical assets, and intellectual property. Wealth provides individuals and organizations with the means to acquire goods and services, invest in opportunities, and achieve their goals.

Economic Goods

Economic goods are goods or services that are obtained through economic activity and are scarce, meaning that they have value and can be bought and sold in markets. Economic goods can be tangible, such as food, clothing, and shelter, or intangible, such as education, healthcare, and entertainment. The production, distribution, and consumption of economic goods are critical components of economic activity.

Free Goods

Free goods, on the other hand, are goods or services that are not limited or scarce. Examples of free goods include air, sunlight, and seawater. Free goods are not typically bought and sold in markets, as they are abundant and available to everyone without any cost. However, free goods can still have value and utility, even if they do not have a market price.

Capital Goods

Capital goods are goods or services that are used to produce other goods or services. Examples of capital goods include machinery, equipment, and raw materials. Capital goods are critical components of production, as they enable businesses to produce goods and services efficiently and effectively. Capital goods are typically durable and can be used multiple times in the production process.

Consumer Goods

Consumer goods, in contrast, are goods or services that are consumed immediately by people. Examples of consumer goods include food, clothing, and entertainment. Consumer goods are produced for the purpose of satisfying human wants and needs, and they are typically bought and sold in markets.

Cost

Cost is a critical concept in economics that refers to the expense of production. Cost includes the costs of raw materials, labor, and other inputs that are used to produce goods or services. Cost can be fixed or variable, depending on the level of production. Understanding cost is essential for businesses, as it helps them to determine the price of their products and services and to make informed decisions about production and investment.

Price

Price is the amount of money obtained in exchange for a good or service. It is the value that buyers are willing to pay for a product or service, and it plays a crucial role in determining the demand and supply of goods and services in a market. Price is influenced by a variety of factors, including supply and demand, competition, and consumer preferences. Understanding price is essential for businesses, as it helps them to determine their revenue and profitability and to make informed decisions about production and investment.

Economic Systems

The way in which humans utilize their environment to satisfy their needs gives rise to various economic systems. These systems can be categorized into three main types:

Collective Economy

In a collective economy, people directly use natural resources without making any significant alterations to them. Examples of collective economies include gathering fruits and nuts, living in caves or trees, and hunting. This type of economy is often associated with primitive or traditional societies.

Simple Transformative Economy

A simple transformative economy involves the accumulation of capital goods for further production. This type of economy is characterized by the use of basic tools and techniques, such as digging sticks and plows, and the domestication of animals. Hunters and agriculturalists often use this type of economy.

Complex Transformative Economy

A complex transformative economy is more advanced and is typically followed by literate societies. This type of economy has two stages:

Early Industrialization: This stage is characterized by the development of more advanced tools and techniques, and the growth of industries.

Modern Industrialism: This stage is marked by the widespread use of advanced technologies, such as machinery and automation, and the development of complex industrial systems.

Overall, economic systems have evolved over time, from simple collective economies to more complex transformative economies. Each type of economy has its own unique characteristics and is shaped by the social, cultural, and technological context in which it operates.

Economic Activities

Economic activities are the backbone of any society, driving growth, development, and prosperity. They encompass a wide range of actions and processes that involve the production, distribution, exchange, and consumption of goods and services.

1. Production

Production is the process of creating goods and services that meet the needs and wants of individuals and societies. It involves combining various factors of production, including:

- Land: Natural resources, such as soil, minerals, and water, that are used to produce goods and services.
- Labour: The physical and mental efforts of individuals that are used to produce goods and services.
- Capital: The tools, machines, buildings, and other equipment used to produce goods and services.
- Entrepreneurship: The organization and management of production, including the taking of risks and the allocation of resources.

Production can take many forms, including manufacturing, agriculture, and services. It is a critical component of economic activity, as it provides the goods and services that individuals and societies need to survive and thrive.

2. Consumption

Consumption is the use of goods and services to satisfy human wants and needs. It is the ultimate goal of economic activity, as individuals and societies produce goods and services in order to consume them. Consumption can be categorized into:

- Necessities: Goods and services that are essential for survival, such as food, clothing, and shelter.
- Comforts: Goods and services that provide comfort and convenience, such as entertainment and travel.
- Luxuries: Goods and services that are desirable but not essential, such as fine dining and luxury goods.

Consumption plays a crucial role in driving economic activity, as it creates demand for goods and services and influences production decisions.

3. Distribution

Distribution refers to the allocation of the value of goods and services among the factors of production. It involves the payment of rewards to the owners of the factors of production, including:

- Wages: The payment to labourers for their work.

- Rent: The payment to landlords for the use of their land and property.

- Interest: The payment to capitalists for the use of their capital.

- Profits: The reward to entrepreneurs for their role in organizing production and taking risks.

Distribution is a critical component of economic activity, as it determines the income of individuals and households and influences their ability to consume goods and services. It is also closely tied to issues of inequality and poverty, as the distribution of income and wealth can have a significant impact on social and economic outcomes.

Modern Economic Institutions: Property

Property, in Hobhouse's phrase, 'is to be conceived in terms of the control of man over things', a control which is recognized by society, more or less permanent, and exclusive. Property may be private (individual or collective) or common.

In his account of the development of property, Hobhouse observed that there is some personal private property in all societies, but that in many primitive societies the principal economic resources are communally owned (e.g., hunting land, grazing land, pasture). In more developed agricultural societies, private ownership comes to predominate. But Hobhouse pointed out that although tribal common ownership disappears, common ownership may be maintained for the joint family.

R.H. Lowie, in an excellent short account of property, which uses much comparative material from primitive and civilized societies, presents much the same view. There is personal private property among all primitive peoples, including names, dances, songs, myths, ceremonial regalia, gifts, weapons, and household implements.

So far as the 'instruments of production' are concerned, there are differences between hunters and food-gatherers, where the land is tribal property (not always well-defined), and agriculturalists and pastoralists. Among agriculturalists, individual private property in land is frequently found, though the clan or tribe may still exercise some control over its use or alienation. In the case of pastoralists, land may be communally owned but not the livestock; 'the ownership of livestock strongly develops the sense of individual property'.

Common ownership by a joint family occurs in many societies. In Europe, the Yugoslav Zadruga was a well-known example, but there were similar forms of property in other peasant societies. Most of these had given place to individual ownership by the early twentieth century.

The nature of property rights in the Hindu joint family in the Vedic period is not entirely clear. Macdonell and Keith argued that (Vedic) passages all negative the idea that the property of the family was family property: it is clear that it was the property of the head of the house, usually the father, and that other members of the family only had moral claims the father could ignore upon it.

There are different types of property, including private property and public property. The property owned by a person or a group of persons is called private property. The public property is the property in the name of a political collectivity, i.e., the State or some part of the State.

Types of Property

Property can be categorized into different types based on ownership and control. The two main types of property are:

1. Private Property

Private property refers to assets or resources owned by individuals or groups of individuals. This type of property is characterized by exclusive ownership and control, where the owner has the right to use, sell, or transfer the property as they see fit. Examples of private property include:

- Personal belongings, such as cars, homes, and jewelry
- Businesses and companies owned by individuals or groups
- Land and real estate owned by private individuals or companies

2. Public Property

Public property, on the other hand, refers to assets or resources owned by the state or a political collectivity. This type of property is typically managed and controlled by government agencies or public authorities, and is intended for the benefit of the general public. Examples of public property include:

- Public parks and recreational facilities
- Government buildings and infrastructure, such as roads and bridges
- Public utilities, such as water and electricity supply systems

In summary, private property is owned and controlled by individuals or groups, while public property is owned and managed by the state or public authorities for the benefit of the general public.

Characteristics of Property

Property has several key characteristics that define its nature and implications. These characteristics include:

1. Transferability

Property can be transferred from one person to another through various means, such as sale, gift, or inheritance. This allows property owners to dispose of their property as they see fit.

2. Separation of Ownership and Use

The owner of the property is not necessarily the user of it. This means that property owners can choose to use their property themselves or allow others to use it in exchange for payment or other forms of compensation.

3. Concrete External Object

Property typically refers to tangible, external objects such as land, buildings, goods, and natural resources. These objects can be physical or immovable, and their ownership can be transferred or sold.

4. Power and Control

Property ownership confers a certain amount of power and control over the property. This includes the right to:

- Use the property as desired
- Exclude others from using the property
- Transfer or sell the property
- Modify or improve the property

5. Collective Agreements and Legitimate Authority

Property rights are based on collective agreements and are backed by legitimate forms of power and authority. This means that property rights are:

- Recognized and protected by law
- Shaped by social norms and expectations
- Enforced by government agencies and institutions

These characteristics highlight the complex nature of property and how it is shaped by social, economic, and political factors. Understanding these characteristics is essential for analyzing property rights and their implications in different contexts.

In addition, property rights can vary across different societies and cultures, and can be influenced by factors such as:

- Cultural norms and values
- Economic systems and institutions
- Political systems and policies

By understanding these factors, we can gain a deeper appreciation for the complexities of property rights and how they shape our relationships with others and with the physical world.

Contract: An Important Economic Institution

A contract is a fundamental economic institution that facilitates trade, commerce, and social interactions. It's an agreement between two or more parties to behave in a particular manner for a specific period.

Definition of Contract

A contract is an enforceable covenant or agreement between two or more persons, with a lawful consideration or cause. This means that a contract is a binding agreement that is recognized and enforced by law.

Characteristics of Contract

1. Competent Parties: A contract is between two or more persons who are competent to contract, meaning they have the capacity to enter into a binding agreement. This includes individuals who are of sound mind, age, and legal capacity.

2. Lawful Consideration: There must be a lawful consideration, which means something of value is exchanged between the parties.

This can include money, goods, services, or promises.

3. Voluntary Agreement: The contract is made voluntarily by the parties, without coercion or duress. This means that both parties must agree to the terms of the contract freely and without pressure.

4. Impersonal Relationship: Contractual relationships are impersonal, meaning they're based on the terms of the agreement rather than personal relationships. This allows parties to enter into agreements with strangers or acquaintances.

5. Limited to Formal Terms: The contractual relationships are limited to the formal terms and conditions specified in the contract. This means that parties are bound by the terms of the agreement, and any disputes will be resolved based on those terms.

6. Time, Place, and Reference: Contractual relationships are limited in terms of time, place, and reference, meaning they're specific to a particular context. This helps to clarify the scope of the agreement and prevent misunderstandings.

7. Rational: Contractual relations are rational, meaning they're based on reason and calculation. This allows parties to make informed decisions and negotiate agreements that benefit both parties.

Types of Contracts

1. Express Contract: An express contract is a written or oral agreement where the terms are explicitly stated.

2. Implied Contract: An implied contract is an agreement that is inferred from the actions or circumstances of the parties.

3. Unilateral Contract: A unilateral contract is an agreement where one party makes a promise in exchange for the other party's action.

Importance of Contract

Contracts play a crucial role in facilitating trade and commerce by providing a framework for agreements between parties. They help to:

- Establish clear expectations and obligations
- Reduce uncertainty and risk
- Provide a basis for resolving disputes

- Facilitate economic growth and development

In summary, contracts are a vital economic institution that enables parties to enter into agreements and conduct business with confidence. By understanding the characteristics and importance of contracts, we can appreciate their role in shaping economic activity and social interactions.

Corporation: A Modern Economic Institution

A corporation is a modern form of economic organization that has evolved from the joint stock company. It's a device that allows small amounts of money to be pooled together to create a larger amount, facilitating large-scale economic activity. According to Justice Marshall, "A corporation is an artificial being, invisible, intangible and existing only in contemplation of law." It's a legal entity that exists separately from its individual members, with its own rights and obligations.

A corporation is characterized by its ability to exist in perpetuity, unaffected by the death or resignation of its individual members. It's legally authorized to act as a single person, allowing it to enter into contracts, own property, and engage in economic activity. However, a corporation can have no legal existence outside the boundaries of the sovereignty by which it is created.

The corporation has several advantages, including the ability to pool resources, limit liability, and exist in perpetuity. These characteristics make it an attractive form of economic organization for businesses and investors. Corporations play a crucial role in modern economies, enabling large-scale economic activity, innovation, and growth. They facilitate economic development, job creation, and investment opportunities, making them a vital part of modern economic systems.

Types of Corporation

Corporations can be categorized into two main types: Corporation Aggregate and Corporation Sole. Understanding the differences between these two types is essential for grasping the complexities of corporate law and structure.

1. Corporation Aggregate

A Corporation Aggregate is a corporation consisting of several persons united into one body. This type of corporation has a perpetual existence without change, meaning that an estate once vested in it continues to be vested without interruption. In other words, the corporation's existence is not affected by changes in its membership.

Examples of Corporation Aggregates include:

- Companies registered under Company Law

- Joint-stock companies

- Cooperative societies

Corporation Aggregates are often used for business purposes, allowing multiple individuals to come together to form a single entity that can own property, enter into contracts, and engage in economic activity.

2. Corporation Sole

A Corporation Sole, on the other hand, is a corporation consisting of a single person who is made a body corporate and politic. This type of corporation is typically created to give the individual certain legal capacities and advantages, such as perpetuity, which they would not have as an individual.

Examples of Corporation Sole include:

- The Sovereign of England

- Bishops

- Deans

- Vicars

In the case of a Corporation Sole, the corporation's existence is tied to the office, rather than the individual holding it. When the individual holding the office dies or resigns, the position is in abeyance until a successor is appointed. This means that the corporation's existence continues uninterrupted, despite changes in the individual holding the office.

Corporation Sole is often used for ecclesiastical or governmental purposes, where a single individual holds a unique office or position.

Key Differences

The key differences between Corporation Aggregate and Corporation Sole are:

- Number of Members: Corporation Aggregate consists of multiple members, while Corporation Sole consists of a single individual.

- Purpose: Corporation Aggregate is often used for business purposes, while Corporation Sole is used for ecclesiastical or governmental purposes.

- Existence: Corporation Aggregate has a perpetual existence without change, while Corporation Sole's existence is tied to the office, rather than the individual holding it.

Understanding these differences is essential for navigating the complexities of corporate law and structure.

Economic Systems

Human beings crossed the stage of dependence on nature for their food and shelter. They started to use tools for collecting food and for hunting animals. They started to cultivate crops and then reached the industrial stage. All these activities are considered economic systems and they became sub-systems of society.

Types of Economic Systems

The economic systems may be classified as below:

1. The Primitive Economic System: At the beginning, there is the 'collective economy system'. Here, the direct use of the product of nature without making any alteration in them is adopted by the people, e.g., collection of fruits, nuts, roots, and living in caves, under trees, or in the open air. Stage by stage, people started hunting and cattle rearing and a modicum of agriculture. Their tools and technology were very simple and crude. Their economic activities were dependent on the weather conditions. They were nomads. Their tools may have included the bow and arrow for hunting and plough and hoe for agriculture.

Features of the Primitive Economic System

- Interconnected Activities: The economic, religious, and magical activities are intertwined, meaning that these activities were not separate or distinct. For example, hunting and gathering were not just economic activities but also had spiritual significance.

- No Profit Motive: There is a complete absence of desire for making profit, as the focus is on survival rather than accumulation of wealth. People in primitive societies were more concerned with meeting their basic needs than accumulating wealth.

- No Monetary System: There is no money involvement, and economic activities are based on bartering or sharing. People exchanged goods and services without using money.

- Collective Ownership: The wealth was not accumulated by individuals for any material objective and exchange, as the focus is on meeting basic needs rather than accumulating wealth. Property is not privately owned, but belongs to the group or community.

- Division of Labor: The division of labor is based on sex, with different roles and responsibilities assigned to men and women. For example, men may have been responsible for hunting, while women gathered fruits and roots.

Evolution of Economic Systems

As societies evolved, so did their economic systems. The development of science and technology introduced mechanization in agriculture, leading to the Green Revolution. This transformed the nature of agriculture and increased food production.

- Mechanization in Agriculture: High-power tractors for tilling the land, high-efficiency tube wells and canals for irrigation, and high-efficiency harvesters for threshing grains increased agricultural productivity. This led to increased food production and reduced manual labor.

- New Tools and Machines: A variety of tools and machines were invented for agriculture, and different types of fertilizers were developed to improve crop yields. These innovations increased agricultural productivity and efficiency.

Characteristics of Modern Economic Systems

The production system became very expensive due to the need for huge capital for purchasing raw materials, machines, and tools and other capital goods. The whole economic system became complex with the arrival of new institutions such as:

- Financing Agencies: Providing financial support for businesses and individuals. These agencies include banks, venture capitalists, and other financial institutions that provide funding for various economic activities.

- Marketing Agencies: Helping businesses to promote and sell their products. These agencies specialize in advertising, branding, and other marketing activities that help businesses reach their target audience.

- Transportation and Communication Systems: Facilitating the movement of goods, services, and information. These systems include roads, railways, airports, seaports, and digital communication networks that enable fast and efficient exchange of goods and services.

Other characteristics of modern economic systems include:

- Increased Division of Labor and Specialization: As economies grew, people began to specialize in specific tasks, leading to increased efficiency and productivity. This specialization has led to the development of new industries and occupations.

- Urbanization and New Social Problems: The growth of cities led to new social problems such as slum-dwelling and insecurity. Urbanization has also led to increased economic opportunities and cultural diversity.

- Government Intervention: The State has to take up welfare measures such as establishment of schools, hospitals, public gardens, etc. to address social problems and provide essential services. Governments play a crucial role in regulating economic activity and providing public goods.

- Expansion in Arts, Science, and Literacy: Modern economic systems have led to significant advancements in arts, science, and literacy, driving innovation and progress. These advancements have improved the quality of life and increased economic opportunities.

In summary, economic systems have evolved significantly over time, from primitive to modern industrial societies. Understanding the characteristics and evolution of economic systems is essential for analyzing the complexities of modern economies. By examining the different stages of economic development, we can gain insights into the challenges and opportunities faced by societies at different levels of economic development.

Types of Modern Economy

Types of economy may be classified as:

(i) the feudal;

(ii) the capitalist;

(iii) the socialist; and

(iv) the mixed economy.

(1) The Feudal Economy

The feudal or manorial system consisted of a vast extent of arable land ruled over by feudal lords and cultivated by their tenants who were either serfs or freeman. The manor was practically a self-contained unit made up of land cultivators. The rise of towns was favourable to the serfs who could obtain their freedom, the feudal system gave way to the guild system. The emergence of factory system led to the development of modern economic system-capitalism and socialism.

(2) The Capitalist Economy

Sidney Webb defines capitalism as a particular economic system where a small part of the population of a society owns and controls the organization of the land, machinery and labour force of the community, and the bulk of the workers who do not own the means of production become wage earners. Prof. Locks says, "Capitalism is a system of economic organization featured by the private ownership and the use for private profit of man-made and nature-made capital."

(3) The Socialist Economy

In a socialist economy, the means of production are owned and controlled by the state or by the workers themselves. The goal of a socialist economy is to promote economic equality and social welfare.

(4) The Mixed Economy

A mixed economy combines elements of both capitalist and socialist economies. In a mixed economy, private enterprises coexist with government intervention and regulation.

Features of Capitalist Economy or Capitalism

Capitalism is characterized by several key features, including:

1. Competition: Producers compete with one another to get the consumer's choice, driving innovation and efficiency.

2. Laissez-Faire: The free enterprise system operates without significant governmental interference, allowing businesses to make decisions based on market forces.

3. Consumer Sovereignty: Under capitalism, the consumer is sovereign, meaning that their preferences and demands drive production and economic activity.

4. Market Forces: The demand and supply of goods and services determine their prices in the market, influencing production and consumption decisions.

5. Private Property: Everybody has the right to acquire, keep, and pass on private property to their heirs or dispose of it as they see fit.

6. Freedom to Form Businesses: Every citizen has the right to form any firm or company anywhere they like, promoting entrepreneurship and economic growth.

7. Profit Motive: The pursuit of profit induces people to undertake production activities, driving innovation and economic development.

8. Income Inequality: Capitalism can lead to significant inequalities of wealth and income in society, as those who are more successful in business may accumulate more wealth.

9. Class Division: The society is often divided into two classes - the 'haves' and 'have nots' - which can lead to social and economic tensions.

10. Entrepreneurial Direction: The entire production of a commodity is under the direction of the entrepreneur, who makes decisions about production, pricing, and distribution.

11. Risk and Reward: There are risks of losses along with the potential for attractive profits under capitalism, making it a system that rewards risk-taking and innovation.

Merits of Capitalism

The capitalist system has several merits, including:
- Optimum utilization of resources
- Maximization of welfare
- Individual freedom
- Rising standard of living
- Goods available at lower prices
- Reward for risk-taking
- Higher rate of capital formation
- Economic development and prosperity
- Incentives for hard work

Overall, capitalism is a system that promotes economic growth, innovation, and individual freedom, but it also has its drawbacks, such as income inequality and social class divisions.

The Socialist Economy

H.D. Dickenson writes, "Socialism is an economic organisation of society in which the material means of production are owned by the whole community and operated by organs representative of, and responsible to the community according to a general economic plan, all members of the community being entitled to benefits, from the results of such socialised planned production on the basis of equal rights."

Features of Socialist Economy

1. State Ownership of Capital: The capital is in the ownership of the State, ensuring that resources are utilized for the benefit of the community.

2. State Control: The State controls the production and distribution of goods and services, allowing for a coordinated and planned economy.

3. Equal Opportunities: Equal opportunities are provided to all members of society, promoting social and economic equality.

4. Classless Society: Socialism aims to establish a classless society, where everyone has equal rights and opportunities.

5. Equitable Distribution of Income: Equitable distribution of income is an essential feature of socialism, ensuring that everyone has access to a fair share of resources.

6. Centrally Planned Economy: A socialist economy is necessarily a centrally planned economy, where decisions are made by the State or representative organs.

7. Alternative to Capitalism: Socialism is an alternative system to capitalism, offering a different approach to economic organization and resource allocation.

Advantages of Socialist Economy

The advantages of a socialist economy include:
- Equal opportunities for all
- No wastage of resources
- No unearned income
- No exploitation
- Stability of prices
- Full employment
- Social justice
- Increase in national product
- Rapid economic growth
- Economic use of resources

Key Characteristics

1. Public Ownership: Socialism is based on the public ownership of the instruments of production, ensuring that resources are utilized for the benefit of the community.

2. Production for Use: Production is focused on meeting the needs of society rather than generating profits.

1. Restrictions on Private Property: Unrestricted private property would not be allowed, ensuring that resources are utilized for the greater good.

X

Social Stratification

Social stratification is a universal phenomenon that exists in all societies, regardless of their complexity or simplicity. It refers to the horizontal division of society into higher and lower social units, with individuals and groups occupying different positions in a hierarchical structure. According to Raymonds W. Murray, "Social stratification is a horizontal division of society into 'higher' and 'lower' social units." This concept is further reinforced by Sorokin, who points out that "Unstratified society with real equality of its members is a myth which has never been realised in the history of mankind."

Social stratification is characterized by inequality and differences in status, power, and privileges. It can take various forms, including caste systems, class systems, estate systems, and social status based on occupation, education, or income. These forms of stratification can have a significant impact on life chances, opportunities, and experiences. Economic inequality, power relations, social and cultural norms, and historical and institutional factors all contribute to the development and persistence of social stratification.

The consequences of social stratification are far-reaching, leading to inequality, social injustice, limited social mobility, and impact on health, education, and well-being. Those in positions of power and privilege often work to maintain their status and limit access to resources and opportunities for others. Despite efforts to promote equality and challenge social stratification, such as revolutionary ideas and radicalism, equality and democracy, socialism and communism, it remains a persistent feature of many societies.

In conclusion, social stratification is a complex and multifaceted phenomenon that exists in all societies. Understanding its characteristics, forms, causes, and consequences is essential for addressing issues of inequality and promoting social justice. By recognizing the persistence of social stratification, we can work towards creating more equitable and just societies.

Definition of Social Stratification

Social stratification refers to the division of society into permanent groups or categories linked by relationships of superiority and subordination. According to Gilbert, it involves the differentiation of individuals and groups based on recognition and privilege, resulting in the creation of social strata. This concept is further reinforced by other sociologists, including John F. Cuber and William F. Kenkel, who describe social stratification as a pattern of superimposed categories of differential privilege.

Key Features

The key features of social stratification include:
- Inequality and differentiation in status, rank, or privilege
- Hierarchical structure with superior and subordinate positions
- Social strata or categories that are relatively permanent
- Differential treatment and privilege based on social position

Perspectives on Social Stratification

Sociologists have offered various perspectives on social stratification, highlighting its complex and multifaceted nature. Kurt B. Mayer's definition emphasizes the system of differentiation that includes a hierarchy of social positions, with occupants treated as superior, equal, or inferior relative to one another.

Conclusion

In conclusion, social stratification is a complex phenomenon characterized by inequality and differentiation in status, rank, or privilege. Understanding its definition and key features is essential for analyzing social structures and relationships. By recognizing the hierarchical nature of social stratification, we can better comprehend the social dynamics and inequalities that shape our societies.

Forms of Social Stratification

Sociologists have identified four main types of social stratification: slavery, estates, caste, and social class and status. Each of these forms has distinct characteristics and implications for individuals and societies. Slavery is an extreme form of inequality where certain groups of individuals are treated as property, with little to no rights. According to L.T. Hobhouse, a slave is "a man whom law and custom regard as the property of another." Slavery has existed in various forms throughout history, with notable examples including ancient Greece and Rome, and the Southern States of the U.S.A. in the 18th and 19th centuries.

Slavery

The characteristics of slavery include unlimited master power over slaves, where slaves are considered possessions or property, and have no political rights or social status. Slaves are also subjected to compulsory labor, and the basis of slavery is always economic. As H.J. Nieboer noted, the relation between master and slave is properly expressed by the slave being called the master's "possession" or "property." This highlights the extreme nature of slavery, where individuals are treated as commodities rather than human beings.

Slavery has had a profound impact on individuals, societies, and economies. It has led to significant social, economic, and cultural inequalities, and has shaped the course of human history. The legacy of slavery continues to influence contemporary societies, with ongoing issues of racism, discrimination, and social injustice. Understanding the characteristics and impact of slavery is essential for addressing these issues and promoting social justice.

In addition to slavery, the other forms of social stratification, including estates, caste, and social class and status, also have distinct characteristics and implications. Estates refer to a system of stratification where individuals are assigned to different groups based on their ownership of land or other forms of property. Caste systems, on the other hand, are based on hereditary groups that are often associated with specific occupations or social roles. Social class and status refer to the economic and social position of individuals within a society, often determined by factors such as income, education, and occupation.

Overall, understanding the different forms of social stratification is essential for analyzing social structures and relationships. By recognizing the characteristics and implications of each form, we can better comprehend the social dynamics and inequalities that shape our societies.

Estate

The feudal estate system was a basis of social stratification in medieval society, where individuals were categorized based on their ownership of land and their roles within the feudal hierarchy. Those who owned large estates, such as the nobility, held significant power and influence, while those with smaller estates or no estates had limited social status. The feudal estates were legally defined and had specific functions, with the nobility ordained to defend all, the clergy to provide spiritual guidance, and the commons to provide food and economic support. This system was reinforced by laws, customs, and social norms, and it played a significant role in shaping medieval society.

The nobility and clergy held positions of power, while the commons and serfs were subordinate, highlighting the hierarchical structure and unequal distribution of power and resources that characterized the feudal estate system. The nobility's role in defense and military leadership gave them significant authority, while the clergy's role in spiritual guidance gave them influence over the moral and cultural fabric of society. The commons, on the other hand, were responsible for providing the economic foundation of the feudal system, through their labor and production.

This system of social stratification had far-reaching consequences, shaping not only the social and economic structures of medieval society but also the relationships between individuals and groups. It reinforced social norms and expectations, and limited social mobility for those at the lower end of the hierarchy. Despite its limitations, the feudal estate system played a significant role in shaping the course of medieval history, and its legacy can still be seen in the modern-day social and economic structures of many European countries.

Caste System

The Indian caste system is a complex and ancient form of social stratification that has been a defining feature of Indian society for centuries. It is a system of social hierarchy that categorizes individuals into different groups, or castes, based on their birth, occupation, and social status. The caste system is unique in its complexity and rigidity, with individuals often facing significant social and economic consequences for attempting to move outside of their designated caste.

At its core, the caste system is based on the concept of ritual purity and pollution, with different castes being associated with different levels of purity and pollution. The system is often divided into four main varnas, or categories: Brahmins, Kshatriyas, Vaisyas, and Sudras, with each varna having its own distinct roles and responsibilities. However, in reality, the caste system is far more complex, with thousands of sub-castes, or jatis, each with their own unique customs, traditions, and social status.

The caste system has been a source of both social cohesion and conflict, with many individuals and groups working to challenge and reform the system. Despite its complexities and challenges, the caste system remains an important part of Indian society and culture, influencing social relationships, economic opportunities, and cultural practices to this day. Its impact can be seen in many aspects of Indian life, from marriage and family dynamics to education and employment opportunities.

The caste system's influence extends beyond Hindu communities, with many non-Hindu groups also being affected by its social and cultural norms. Understanding the caste system is essential for grasping the complexities of Indian society and culture, and for appreciating the challenges and opportunities faced by individuals and groups within this complex social hierarchy. By examining the caste system, we can gain insights into the social, economic, and cultural dynamics that shape Indian society, and better understand the ways in which social stratification can impact individuals and communities.

The Indian caste system is a complex and ancient form of social stratification that has been a defining feature of Indian society for centuries. It is a system of social hierarchy that categorizes individuals into different groups, or castes, based on their birth, occupation, and social status. The caste system is unique in its complexity and rigidity, with individuals often facing significant social and economic consequences for attempting to move outside of their designated caste.

At its core, the caste system is based on the concept of ritual purity and pollution, with different castes being associated with different levels of purity and pollution. The system is often divided into four main varnas, or categories: Brahmins, Kshatriyas, Vaisyas, and Sudras, with each varna having its own distinct roles and responsibilities. However, in reality, the caste system is far more complex, with thousands of sub-castes, or jatis, each with their own unique customs, traditions, and social status.

Characteristics of the Caste System

- Endogamy: Castes are typically endogamous, meaning that individuals are expected to marry within their own caste.

- Hierarchical grading: Castes are ranked in a hierarchical order based on notions of ritual purity, with higher castes considered purer and less polluted.

- Traditional occupations: Castes are often associated with traditional occupations, such as Brahmins with priestly duties, Kshatriyas with warrior roles, and Vaisyas with trade and commerce.

- Ritual practices: The caste system is deeply tied to ritual practices and notions of purity and pollution, with different castes having different levels of access to sacred spaces and rituals.

Impact of the Caste System

The caste system has had a profound impact on Indian society, shaping social relationships, economic opportunities, and cultural practices. Even non-Hindus, such as Muslims, Christians, Jews, and Parsis, have been influenced by the caste system to some extent. The system has been a source of both social cohesion and conflict, with many individuals and groups working to challenge and reform the system.

Complexity and Variations

The caste system is not uniform across India, with different regions and communities having their own unique caste dynamics. Despite its complexities and challenges, the caste system remains an important part of Indian society and culture, influencing social relationships and economic opportunities to this day. Its impact can be seen in many aspects of Indian life, from marriage and family dynamics to education and employment opportunities.

The caste system's influence extends beyond Hindu communities, with many non-Hindu groups also being affected by its social and cultural norms. Understanding the caste system is essential for grasping the complexities of Indian society and culture, and for appreciating the challenges and opportunities faced by individuals and groups within this complex social hierarchy. By examining the caste system, we can gain insights into the social, economic, and cultural dynamics that shape Indian society, and better understand the ways in which social stratification can impact individuals and communities.

Characteristics of Social Stratification

According to Melvin M. Tumin, social stratification has several key characteristics that shape the social landscape of societies. These characteristics include:

1. Social and Patterned: Social stratification is a social phenomenon that follows a patterned structure, with individuals and groups being ranked in a hierarchical order. This ranking is often based on factors such as wealth, power, prestige, and occupation.

2. Universality: Social stratification is ancient and has been found in all societies, regardless of their size, complexity, or cultural background. This suggests that social stratification is a fundamental aspect of human society, shaped by factors such as economic systems, cultural norms, and historical context.

3. Inequality: Social stratification is characterized by inequality, with individuals and groups having unequal access to resources, power, and prestige. This inequality can lead to social and economic disparities, with some individuals and groups having more opportunities and privileges than others.

4. Diversity in Forms: Social stratification can take many different forms, depending on the society and its cultural, economic, and historical context. For example, some societies may be stratified based on caste, while others may be stratified based on class or economic status.

5. Consequential: Social stratification has significant consequences for individuals and groups, with unequal distribution of valued resources, such as wealth, power, and status, affecting life chances and opportunities. This can lead to social mobility, where individuals or groups move up or down the social ladder, or social exclusion, where certain groups are denied access to resources and opportunities.

Implications of Social Stratification

The characteristics of social stratification have important implications for individuals and societies. Social stratification can:

- Shape social relationships and interactions
- Influence access to education, employment, and healthcare
- Affect social mobility and opportunities for advancement
- Contribute to social inequality and conflict
- Influence cultural norms and values

Understanding the characteristics of social stratification is essential for grasping the complexities of social inequality and its impact on individuals and societies. By examining the ways in which social stratification shapes social relationships and structures, we can gain insights into the ways in which societies can work towards greater equality and social justice.

Key Aspects of Social Stratification

Social stratification is a complex and multifaceted phenomenon that shapes societies in various ways. Here are some key aspects of social stratification:

1. Stratification in Different Forms

Social stratification is not static and can take different forms in various societies. Strata can be arranged in terms of:

- Class: Economic-based stratification, where individuals are ranked according to their income, wealth, and occupation.

- Caste: A rigid, hereditary system of stratification, often based on occupation or social status.

- Estate: A system of stratification based on ownership of land and other forms of property.

These forms help conceptualize the different ways in which strata can be arranged and highlight the differences in degree among strata.

2. Universality and Ubiquity of Stratification

Social stratification is universal and ubiquitous, found in all societies, regardless of their size, complexity, or cultural background. It is present in both:

- Literate societies: Societies with a written language and formal education systems.

- Non-literate societies: Societies without a written language, where social stratification may be based on oral traditions and cultural norms.

Socially prescribed inequalities between men and women, adults and children, and rich and poor are common features of social stratification.

3. Consequences of Stratification

Social stratification has significant consequences for individuals and groups, including:

- Life chances: Access to resources, healthcare, and opportunities that affect one's quality of life and longevity. This can include factors such as:
- Infant mortality rates
- Life expectancy
- Access to education and employment opportunities
- Life-styles: Patterns of consumption, recreation, and cultural participation that reflect one's social position. This can include factors such as:
- Housing and neighborhood quality
- Leisure activities and hobbies
- Cultural and artistic pursuits

These consequences can vary greatly depending on one's position in the social hierarchy.

4. Social Nature of Stratification

Social stratification is determined by social elements such as:

- Education: Access to quality education and training opportunities.
- Skills: Development of skills and expertise that are valued in the labor market.
- Wealth: Ownership of assets and resources that generate income and wealth.
- Occupation: Type of work and occupation, which can affect social status and economic opportunities.

These factors shape an individual's social position, rather than biological characteristics like weight or height.

5. Ancient Roots of Stratification

Social stratification has ancient roots, with evidence of stratification found in past societies. The determinants of stratification have evolved over time, reflecting changes in:

- Societal values: Cultural norms and values that shape social relationships and institutions.

- Economic systems: Modes of production and distribution that affect social inequality.

- Cultural norms: Social and cultural practices that reinforce or challenge social stratification.

Despite these changes, social stratification remains a persistent feature of human societies.

By understanding these key aspects of social stratification, we can gain insights into the complex dynamics of social inequality and its impact on individuals and societies.

Theories of Social Stratification

Social stratification has been a topic of interest for social thinkers and philosophers for centuries. From ancient times to modern era, various theories have been proposed to explain the phenomenon of social stratification.

1. Karl Marx's Theory

Karl Marx's theory of social stratification is one of the most influential and widely discussed theories. According to Marx:

- Class struggle: The history of all hitherto existing societies is the history of class struggle, arising from the division of society into classes with opposite interests.

- Class consciousness: Each class supports a particular class consciousness, giving rise to class conflict between classes with opposite interests.

- Economic determinism: Marx believed that economic factors are the primary drivers of social stratification, with classes emerging based on their relationship to the means of production.

Marx's theory emphasizes the role of economic factors in shaping social stratification and highlights the importance of class conflict in understanding social change.

2. Max Weber's Theory

Max Weber's theory of social stratification builds on and critiques Marx's ideas. According to Weber:

- Multidimensional approach: Weber argued that social stratification is not solely determined by economic factors, but also by social status and power.

- Classes, status groups, and parties: Weber identified three main dimensions of social stratification:
- Classes: economic-based stratification
- Status groups: social-based stratification, including prestige and honor
- Parties: power-based stratification, including access to resources and decision-making
- Life chances: Weber believed that social stratification affects life chances, including access to education, employment, and healthcare.

Weber's theory highlights the complexity of social stratification and the need to consider multiple dimensions when understanding social inequality.

Comparison of Marx and Weber's Theories

While both Marx and Weber's theories address social stratification, they differ in their emphasis and approach:

- Economic determinism vs. multidimensional approach: Marx emphasizes the role of economic factors, while Weber takes a more nuanced approach, considering multiple dimensions of social stratification.

- Class conflict vs. social status: Marx focuses on class conflict, while Weber highlights the importance of social status and power in shaping social stratification.

- Revolution vs. reform: Marx advocates for revolutionary change to address social inequality, while Weber suggests that reform and social mobility can help mitigate the effects of social stratification.

Implications of Social Stratification Theories

Theories of social stratification have important implications for understanding social inequality and its effects on individuals and societies. By examining the different approaches and perspectives, we can:

- Identify the root causes of social inequality: Understanding the underlying factors that contribute to social stratification can help us develop effective strategies for addressing inequality.

- Develop policies and interventions: Theories of social stratification can inform policies and interventions aimed at reducing social inequality and promoting social mobility.

- Promote social justice and equality: By understanding the complex dynamics of social stratification, we can work towards creating a more just and equitable society.

Applications of Social Stratification Theories

Theories of social stratification can be applied in various fields, including:

- Sociology: Understanding social stratification is essential for sociologists to analyze social structures and relationships.

- Policy-making: Policymakers can use theories of social stratification to develop policies that address social inequality and promote social mobility.

- Education: Educators can use theories of social stratification to understand the impact of social inequality on educational outcomes and opportunities.

By exploring the theories of social stratification, we can gain a deeper understanding of the complex social structures that shape our lives and societies.

Gerhard Lenski's Distribution Theory

Gerhard Lenski's distribution theory provides valuable insights into the dynamics of social stratification and inequality. According to Lenski:

- Scarcity of resources: No society is perfect, and every society faces scarcity of material and non-material resources.

- Unequal capacity: Individuals have unequal capacity to own and access these scarce resources, leading to social inequality.

Lenski proposes two types of distribution:

1. Distribution based on Labor and Cooperation

- Sharing the fruits of labor: In societies where production is primarily based on individual labor and cooperation, distribution is often based on the principle of sharing the fruits of labor for survival and livelihood.

- Reciprocity and mutual aid: This type of distribution is often characterized by reciprocity and mutual aid, where individuals share resources and expertise to ensure collective well-being.

2. Distribution based on Power and Surplus Production

- Power dynamics: When societies develop technological capacity and produce surpluses, power becomes a determining factor in the distribution of these surpluses.

- Inequality and social stratification: Those with more power and influence tend to accumulate more resources, leading to social inequality and stratification.

- Exploitation and dominance: This type of distribution can lead to exploitation and dominance, where those with power use their position to accumulate more resources and maintain their privileged position.

Implications of Lenski's Theory

Lenski's distribution theory has significant implications for understanding social inequality and stratification:

- Power and resource distribution: The distribution of power and resources plays a crucial role in shaping social stratification and inequality.

- Technological advancements: Technological advancements can lead to increased production and surpluses, but also create new forms of social inequality and stratification.

- Social change and mobility: Understanding the dynamics of power and resource distribution can help us identify opportunities for social change and mobility.

Applications of Lenski's Theory

Lenski's distribution theory can be applied in various fields, including:

- Sociology: Understanding the dynamics of power and resource distribution can help sociologists analyze social structures and relationships.

- Economics: Lenski's theory can inform economic policies and interventions aimed at reducing social inequality and promoting social mobility.

- Anthropology: Anthropologists can use Lenski's theory to study the distribution of resources and power in different cultures and societies.

By examining Lenski's distribution theory, we can gain a deeper understanding of the complex dynamics of social stratification and inequality, and how they shape our lives and societies.

Theories of Social Stratification -II

1. Conservative or Status Quo View

- Opposition to change: Conservatives oppose changes and prefer the status quo, believing that the existing system is desirable and doesn't need alteration.

- Support for existing power structures: This view supports existing power structures, such as slavery and private property, which are bases for stratification.

- Justification of inequality: Conservatives often justify inequality by arguing that it is natural or necessary for social order.

- Examples: Aristotle's views on slavery and social hierarchy are an example of the conservative perspective.

2. Darwinist View

- Evolutionary selection: Followers of Charles Darwin believe that evolutionary selection makes the more talented do better than the less talented.

- Natural differences: This view posits that natural differences among people are reflected in unequal social positions.

- Meritocracy: Darwinists often argue that social stratification is a meritocracy, where the most talented and capable individuals rise to the top.

- Critique: Critics argue that this view oversimplifies the complexity of social stratification and ignores the role of privilege and opportunity.

3. Gaetano Mosca's Theory

- Inevitability of inequality: Mosca proposed that the essentials of political organization in a society inevitably produce inequalities in social power.

- Division between elites and commoners: Society is divided between the "elites" and the "commoners," with the dominant class controlling economic privileges.

- Power dynamics: Mosca's theory highlights the importance of power dynamics in shaping social stratification.

- Implications: Mosca's theory implies that social mobility is limited, and that those born into privileged positions are more likely to maintain their status.

4. Functional Theory

- Essential and inevitable: Functionalists believe that stratification is essential and inevitable for both individuals and society.

- Allocation based on capacity: Functions should be allocated to individuals based on their capacities.

- Social order: Functionalists argue that social stratification promotes social order and stability by ensuring that the most qualified individuals occupy important positions.

- Critique: Critics argue that this theory doesn't account for the role of force in establishing and maintaining systems of stratification, and ignores issues of inequality and injustice.

5. Conflict Theory

- Inequality and conflict: Conflict theorists believe that inequality in society leads to conflict, and there's no guarantee that high social positions will be filled by highly qualified persons.

- Force and privilege: Those with power and privilege use force, deception, or birth to occupy higher social positions, limiting opportunities for others.

- Exploitation: Conflict theorists argue that social stratification leads to exploitation, where the dominant class exploits the subordinate class.

- Social change: Conflict theorists believe that social change can only be achieved through the redistribution of power and resources.

Comparison of Theories

Each theory provides a unique perspective on social stratification, highlighting different aspects of the phenomenon.

While some theories justify inequality, others critique it and advocate for social change.

Implications of Theories

Understanding these theories can provide insights into the mechanisms that shape social inequality and stratification. By examining the different perspectives, we can:

- Identify the root causes of social inequality: Understanding the underlying factors that contribute to social stratification can help us develop effective strategies for addressing inequality.

- Develop policies and interventions: Theories of social stratification can inform policies and interventions aimed at reducing social inequality and promoting social mobility.

- Promote social justice and equality: By understanding the complex dynamics of social stratification, we can work towards creating a more just and equitable society.

Conclusion

Theories of social stratification provide a framework for understanding the complex dynamics of social inequality. By examining the different perspectives, we can gain insights into the mechanisms that shape social stratification and develop effective strategies for promoting social justice and equality.

XI
Status and Role

Status refers to the position or rank that an individual holds within a given social system. It is a complex concept that encompasses various aspects, including prestige, respect, and influence. According to various sociologists, status can be defined as a position in the general institutional system, a location within a group, or a rank-order position assigned by a group to a role or set of roles.

The status of a person is based on social evaluations, and it can be high or low depending on the importance of the role they play in the group. Status grants certain prerogatives and privileges, and it is essential for promoting responsibility, maintaining a balanced and integrated personality, and furthering material possessions.

There are six factors that determine an individual's status, according to Parsons. These factors include birth, possessions, personal qualities, personal achievement, power, and authority. Status is a vital aspect of social relationships, and it plays a significant role in shaping individual behavior and interactions within society.

Social inequality is closely linked to status, and it is an unconsciously evolved device by which societies ensure that the most important positions are filled by the most qualified persons. Every society, regardless of its complexity, must differentiate persons in terms of both prestige and esteem.

In various societies, status has been used to grant privileges and exemptions to certain groups or individuals. For example, in feudal societies, feudal lords were often not punished for certain crimes due to their higher social status. Similarly, in Indian society, Brahmins were accorded a higher status and privileges for a significant period.

Overall, status is a crucial aspect of social life, and it plays a significant role in shaping individual behavior and social relationships. Understanding the concept of status and its significance can provide valuable insights into the workings of society and the ways in which individuals interact with each other.

Types of Status

There are two main types of status: Ascribed Status and Achieved Status.

Ascribed Status

Ascribed status refers to the status that is assigned to an individual based on their birth, family background, or social group. This type of status is usually fixed at birth and is not based on individual effort or achievement. Ascribed status can include factors such as:

- Family background: An individual's family background can influence their ascribed status, with certain families or castes holding higher social standing than others.

- Sex: An individual's sex can also influence their ascribed status, with certain societies assigning different roles and expectations to men and women.

- Age: An individual's age can also be a factor in determining their ascribed status, with certain ages being associated with greater respect or authority.

- Kinship: An individual's kinship ties can also influence their ascribed status, with certain family relationships being considered more important or prestigious than others.

Ascribed status can have a significant impact on an individual's life, shaping their opportunities, expectations, and social interactions.

Achieved Status

Achieved status, on the other hand, refers to the status that an individual earns through their own personal efforts and achievements. This type of status is based on individual merit and accomplishment, and it can change over time. Achieved status can be influenced by factors such as:

- Education: An individual's educational achievements can contribute to their achieved status, with higher levels of education often being associated with greater prestige and respect.

- Professional achievements: An individual's professional accomplishments can also contribute to their achieved status, with certain careers or positions being considered more prestigious than others.

- Leadership roles: An individual's leadership roles or positions of authority can also influence their achieved status, with certain roles being associated with greater respect and influence.

Achieved status can provide individuals with a sense of accomplishment and pride, and it can also open up new opportunities and challenges.

Conclusion

In conclusion, ascribed status and achieved status are two distinct types of status that can shape an individual's identity and position within society. Understanding the differences between these two types of status can provide valuable insights into the ways in which society influences individual behavior and opportunities.

Role

A role refers to the task or behavior expected of an individual in a particular social context. It is a set of socially approved and expected behavior patterns associated with a specific position or status within a group or community. Roles play a crucial part in shaping individual behavior and social interactions, and they provide a way for individuals to contribute to and participate in their communities. According to various sociologists, roles are an essential aspect of social organization, and they involve both duties and privileges.

Definition and Characteristics

A role is defined as a set of socially expected and approved behavior patterns associated with a particular position or status. Ogburn defines role as "A role is a set of socially expected and approved behaviour patterns, consisting of both duties and privileges, associated with a particular position in a group." Roles involve behavior that is expected of an individual in a particular social context, and they are associated with specific positions or statuses within a group or community.

Role and Status

The role is, in fact, the action aspect of status. It includes various types of actions that a person has to perform in accordance with the expectations of society. Roles are closely tied to statuses, and they provide a way for individuals to enact the expected behavior patterns associated with their position or status.

Dynamic Nature of Roles

The concept of role can change over time as ideals, values, and objects change according to the situation. Roles are not fixed and can evolve as societal norms and expectations change. This highlights the dynamic nature of roles and the need for individuals to adapt to changing social contexts.

Importance of Role

Roles are essential to social life, and they play a significant role in shaping individual behavior and social interactions. They provide a way for individuals to contribute to and participate in their communities, and they help to establish social order and stability. By understanding the concept of role, we can gain valuable insights into the workings of society and the ways in which individuals interact with each other.

XII
Social Control

Social control is a fundamental concept in sociology that refers to the ways in which society maintains itself and promotes social order and stability. It involves the use of various mechanisms, including persuasion, restraint, and coercion, to guide human behavior into socially desired channels. Social control operates on multiple levels, including group over group, group over its members, and individuals over their fellows.

The concept of social control is essential for understanding how societies function and how social order is maintained. It enables societies to shape individual and collective behavior, ensuring that people adhere to approved patterns of behavior and norms. Through social control, societies can promote social continuity and stability, even in the face of change and uncertainty.

There are various definitions of social control, but most of them agree that it involves the use of mechanisms to influence behavior and promote conformity to norms and rules. According to Gillin and Gillin, social control is "that system of measures, suggestions, persuasion, restraint, and coercion by whatever means, including physical force, by which a society brings into conformity to the approved pattern of behavior or sub-group or by which a group moulds into conformity its members."

Similarly, G.A. Lundberg and others define social control as "those social behaviors which influence individuals or groups towards conformity to established or desired norms." Kingball Young defines social control as "the use of coercion, force, restraint, suggestion, or persuasion of one group over another or of a group over its members or of persons over others to enforce the prescribed rules of the game."

The key aspects of social control include:

1. Mechanisms of control: Social control involves the use of various mechanisms, such as persuasion, restraint, and coercion, to influence behavior.

2. Conformity to norms: Social control aims to promote conformity to established norms and rules, ensuring that individuals and groups behave in ways that are deemed acceptable by society.

3. Multiple levels of control: Social control operates on multiple levels, including group over group, group over its members, and individuals over their fellows.

4. Social order and stability: Social control is essential for maintaining social order and stability, as it enables societies to shape individual and collective behavior and promote conformity to norms and rules.

In conclusion, social control is a vital aspect of social life, as it enables societies to maintain social order and stability. By understanding the mechanisms and processes of social control, we can gain insights into how societies function and how social behavior is shaped.

Mechanisms of Social Control

Social control operates through various mechanisms, including:

Importance of Social Control

Social control is essential for maintaining social order and stability. Without effective social control, societies may experience chaos, disorder, and disintegration. By understanding the functions and mechanisms of social control, we can appreciate its critical role in shaping individual behavior and promoting collective welfare.

Conclusion

In conclusion, social control is a vital aspect of social life, as it enables societies to maintain social order and stability. By understanding the key aspects, functions, and mechanisms of social control, we can gain insights into how societies function and how individual behavior is shaped. Social control is essential for promoting collective welfare and ensuring social cohesion, and its importance cannot be overstated.

Functions of Social Control

Social control serves several critical functions in society, including:

1. Maintaining Social Order

Social control helps maintain the existing social order by enforcing norms, values, and expectations. This ensures that individuals conform to societal expectations, preventing chaos and disorder. Social order is maintained through various mechanisms, such as:

- Laws and Regulations: Laws and regulations provide a framework for behavior, outlining what is acceptable and what is not. For example, traffic laws regulate driving behavior, ensuring road safety.

- Social Norms: Social norms, such as norms around dress code and behavior in public places, help regulate individual behavior and maintain social order.

- Institutional Control: Institutions, such as schools and workplaces, have rules and regulations that maintain social order and ensure that individuals conform to expectations.

2. Establishing Social Unity

By promoting conformity to social norms, social control helps establish social unity and cohesion within groups and communities. When individuals share common values and norms, they are more likely to work together and cooperate. Social unity is achieved through:

- Shared Values and Norms: Shared values and norms create a sense of belonging and identity among individuals, promoting social unity.

- Group Cohesion: Group cohesion is strengthened when individuals work together towards a common goal, promoting social unity and cooperation.

- Social Integration: Social integration occurs when individuals from different backgrounds come together, sharing common values and norms, and working towards a common goal.

3. Regulating Individual Behavior

Social control regulates individual behavior, preventing chaos and disorder in society. By setting boundaries and expectations, social control helps individuals understand what is expected of them and what behavior is acceptable. Individual behavior is regulated through:

- Socialization: Socialization is the process by which individuals learn social norms, values, and expectations, helping them conform to societal expectations.

- Reward and Punishment: Reward and punishment are used to reinforce acceptable behavior and discourage unacceptable behavior.

- Social Pressure: Social pressure from family, friends, and community can influence individual behavior, promoting conformity to social norms.

4. Providing Social Sanction

Social control provides social sanction to approved behaviors and norms, encouraging individuals to conform to societal expectations. When individuals conform to social norms, they are often rewarded with social approval and acceptance. Social sanction is provided through:

- Social Approval: Social approval is given to individuals who conform to social norms, reinforcing acceptable behavior.

- Social Recognition: Social recognition, such as awards and accolades, is given to individuals who make significant contributions to society, promoting social norms and values.

- Social Support: Social support from family, friends, and community provides individuals with a sense of belonging and identity, promoting conformity to social norms.

5. Checking Cultural Maladjustment

Social control helps individuals adjust to changing social environments and cultural norms, preventing cultural maladjustment and social disintegration. By promoting cultural adaptation, social control ensures that individuals can navigate different social contexts effectively. Cultural maladjustment is checked through:

- Cultural Orientation: Cultural orientation programs help individuals adjust to new cultural norms and expectations, promoting cultural adaptation.

- Social Support: Social support from family, friends, and community helps individuals navigate different social contexts, promoting cultural adaptation.

- Education and Training: Education and training programs provide individuals with the skills and knowledge necessary to adapt to changing social environments and cultural norms.

Mechanisms of Social Control

1. Control by Art and Literature: Art and literature have a profound impact on human behavior, shaping our imagination and influencing our actions. They can inspire and shape our imagination, foster a sense of community and shared identity, and even influence our buying behavior through advertisements. The relationship between art and literature and national life is complex, reflecting the values, norms, and experiences of a particular period.

2. Control through Leadership: Leadership plays a crucial role in shaping individual behavior and promoting social control. Leaders provide guidance and direction, channel the functions of a group or organization, and inspire loyalty and devotion, promoting conformity to social norms and expectations. Effective leaders possess natural qualities such as strength of will, imagination, and eloquence, which supplement their authority.

3. Social Control through Intellectual Factors: Intellectual factors, such as reasoning and reflection, play a significant role in shaping individual behavior and promoting social control.

Individuals consider the consequences of their actions, reflect on social norms, and think about their reputation, influencing their behavior and promoting conformity. This intellectual process helps individuals understand the extent of social punishment for violating social codes of conduct and behavior.

4. Social Control through Education: Education is a powerful vehicle for social control, shaping individual behavior and promoting conformity to social norms. It provides moral and intellectual continuity, promotes a social vision of uniformity, and fits individuals for their social role, influencing their behavior and promoting social cohesion. Education links individuals to their heritage and sets a perspective before them, giving them a sense of social responsibility.

5. Social Control through Law: Law is a highly specialized and effective mechanism of social control, providing a framework for behavior and promoting social order. It enforces social norms, punishes deviance, and protects society from harm, promoting social cohesion and stability. Law empowers the executive government to punish those who violate established social orders and encourages those who act rightly and cooperatively.

6. Family: Family plays a significant role in shaping individual behavior and promoting conformity to social norms.

7. Education: Education is another important mechanism of social control, as it teaches individuals about social norms, values, and expectations.

8. Media: Media, including television, social media, and newspapers, can influence individual behavior and promote conformity to social norms.

9. Social institutions: Social institutions, such as government, law, and economy, also play a crucial role in shaping individual behavior and promoting social control.

10. Social Control by Physical Force

Physical force is an important instrument of social control, particularly in maintaining law and order in society. The fear of punishment is a great deterrent that prevents people from violating social norms and encourages them to conform to social expectations. The police, army, and other law enforcement agencies are all instruments of physical force that play a crucial role in maintaining social control.

11. Control through Religion

Religion is a powerful mechanism of social control that influences people's behavior and promotes conformity to social norms. The fear of divine retribution and the desire to please a higher power motivate individuals to behave in ways that are deemed acceptable by society. Religion supports social morality, promotes useful traditions and rites, and provides a sense of community and shared identity.

12. Control through Morals

Moral codes and values are essential components of social control, promoting peace and harmony in society. Morality is closely associated with religious belief, but it has also evolved to become more social and concerned with social justice. Moral codes provide a framework for behavior, guiding individuals to act in ways that are respectful and considerate of others.

13. Control through Family

The family is a fundamental institution of social control, teaching individuals behavior and respect for others from a young age. Family atmosphere and education help individuals learn social norms and values, promoting conformity to social expectations. The family's influence on social control is significant, as it shapes an individual's worldview and behavior.

14. Control through Propaganda

Propaganda is a powerful mechanism of social control that influences people's attitudes and behavior. Through various channels, such as the press, radio, and platform, propaganda can shape public opinion and promote conformity to social norms. Propaganda involves controlling facts and interpretation, using various tactics to persuade individuals to adopt certain views or behaviors.

15. Control through Recreational Group

Recreational groups, such as sports teams and clubs, also play a role in maintaining social control. Games and recreational activities promote social interaction, teamwork, and mutual respect, teaching individuals the importance of cooperation and conformity to rules and norms. Recreational groups provide a platform for socialization, helping individuals develop social skills and values.

These additional mechanisms of social control highlight the complexity and multifaceted nature of social control in shaping individual behavior and promoting conformity to social norms. By understanding these mechanisms, we can gain a deeper appreciation for the ways in which society influences individual behavior and promotes social order.

Types of Social Control

Social control is a complex and multifaceted phenomenon that can be categorized into different types based on various perspectives. Understanding these different types of social control can provide valuable insights into the ways in which society shapes individual behavior and promotes social order.

1. Karl Mannheim's View

Karl Mannheim, a prominent sociologist, has identified two types of social control:

- Direct Social Control: This type of control is found in primary groups such as family, neighborhood, and play groups. In these groups, individuals are directly influenced by the opinions and views of others, and their behavior is controlled by criticism, praise, suggestion, or persuasion. Direct social control is often exercised through face-to-face interactions, where individuals can directly observe and respond to the reactions of others. For example, a child may learn social norms and values through interactions with their parents and siblings.

- Indirect Social Control: This type of control is found in secondary groups, where control is exercised through traditions, institutions, customs, and social mechanisms. The means of social control are often invisible and subtle, and individuals may not even be aware of the control being exercised over them. Indirect social control can be exercised through various channels, such as media, education, and social policies. For instance, social norms and values can be promoted through education, shaping individual behavior and attitudes.

2. Kimball Young's View

Kimball Young, another notable sociologist, has divided social control into two types:

- Positive Social Control: This type of control involves rewarding individuals for conforming to social norms and expectations. Individuals are motivated to behave in certain ways because they receive social recognition, praise, and respect. Positive social control can be exercised through various means, such as awards, recognition, and social approval. For example, an individual may be praised for their volunteer work, encouraging them to continue engaging in such behavior.

- Negative Social Control: This type of control involves discouraging individuals from engaging in certain behaviors through fear of punishment. Punishments can take various forms, including physical, verbal, or social exclusion. Negative social control can be exercised through various means, such as laws, regulations, and social norms. For instance, an individual may be deterred from committing a crime due to the fear of punishment.

3. Other Views

In addition to the above-mentioned types of social control, other forms of social control have been recognized:

- Formal Social Control: This type of control involves institutions and mechanisms that are specifically designed to control behavior, such as government, law, army, and penal codes. Formal social control is often exercised through formal sanctions, such as fines, imprisonment, or other forms of punishment. For example, laws and regulations can be used to control behavior, such as traffic laws or tax laws.

- Informal Social Control: This type of control involves mechanisms that develop informally, such as mores, traditions, and customs. Informal social control can be just as effective as formal social control in shaping individual behavior. For instance, social norms and values can be promoted through social interactions, shaping individual behavior and attitudes.

- Control by Sanction: This type of control involves rewarding individuals for conforming to social norms and punishing those who do not conform. Sanctions can take various forms, including social recognition, praise, or punishment. Control by sanction can be exercised through various means, such as social approval or disapproval. For example, an individual may receive social approval for their charitable work, encouraging them to continue engaging in such behavior.

- Control by Socialization and Education: This type of control involves shaping individual behavior through socialization and education. Individuals learn social norms and values through their interactions with others, and this shapes their behavior and attitudes. Control by socialization and education can be exercised through various means, such as family, education, and media. For instance, children can learn social norms and values through their interactions with their parents and teachers.

Conclusion

In conclusion, social control is a complex and multifaceted phenomenon that can be categorized into different types based on various perspectives. Understanding these different types of social control can provide valuable insights into the ways in which society shapes individual behavior and promotes social order. By recognizing the importance of social control, we can work towards building a more harmonious and cohesive society, where individuals can live and work together in a spirit of cooperation and mutual respect. Effective social control can promote social cohesion, reduce conflict, and improve individual well-being. By understanding the different types of social control, we can develop more effective strategies for promoting social order and improving individual behavior.

XIII

Coercion

Coercion means the use of force or the threat of force to terminate a conflict. Force being an important instrument of social control is as ancient as the society itself. In varying degree, it has been used by all societies. Some societies even now resort to force against the deviants. Traditionally, our political ethics is based on non-violence or least violence. The only state that gave up force and coercion as the instrument of state policy was the Asokan State. Gandhiji made non-violence his weapon, against the strongest empire, the British. In all civilised societies penal codes are reviewed to humanize the law of crime. Force breeds revenge, it does not reform.

The use of coercion in conflict resolution raises important questions about the effectiveness and morality of force as a means of achieving social control. While some societies have relied heavily on coercion to maintain order, others have sought to minimize its use and instead emphasize rehabilitation, restorative justice, and social welfare.

The impact of coercion on individuals and communities can be significant, leading to feelings of resentment, anger, and frustration. In contrast, approaches that prioritize non-violence, empathy, and understanding can help to build trust and promote social cohesion.

As societies continue to evolve and mature, it is likely that the role of coercion in conflict resolution will continue to be reevaluated and refined. By exploring alternative approaches to social control and conflict resolution, we can work towards creating more just and equitable societies for all.

The relationship between coercion, conflict, and social change is complex and multifaceted. Understanding the dynamics of this relationship can help us to develop more effective strategies for promoting social justice and reducing conflict. By prioritizing non-violence, empathy, and understanding, we can work towards creating a more peaceful and harmonious world.

XIV
Conflict

Conflict is a universal phenomenon that occurs in all times and places. It is a social process that arises when individuals or groups have competing interests, values, or goals. A.W. Green defines conflict as "a deliberate attempt to oppose, resist, or coerce the will of another or others." This definition highlights the intentional nature of conflict, where individuals or groups deliberately seek to impose their will on others.

Gillin and Gillin describe conflict as "a social process in which individuals or groups seek their ends by directly challenging the antagonist by violence or threat of violence." This definition emphasizes the role of violence or the threat of violence in conflict, but it's also important to note that conflict can manifest in non-violent forms.

Conflict can take many forms, ranging from subtle and implicit to overt and violent. It involves opposition, hostility, and competition, and can be interpersonal, group, or social in nature. Interpersonal conflict occurs between individuals, while group conflict involves conflicts between different groups or organizations. Social conflict, on the other hand, involves conflicts between different social classes, castes, or communities.

According to Mazumdar, conflict involves "opposition or struggle involving an emotional attitude of hostility as well as violent interference with one's autonomous choice." This definition highlights the emotional and psychological aspects of conflict, where individuals or groups experience feelings of hostility, anger, or frustration.

While conflict is often associated with violence, it can also be non-violent, as seen in civil disobedience and non-violent satyagraha. These forms of conflict resolution emphasize the use of non-violent methods to challenge unjust laws or systems, and can be an effective way to bring about social change.

In conclusion, conflict is a complex and multifaceted phenomenon that can manifest in various forms and contexts. Understanding conflict requires analyzing its causes, dynamics, and consequences, as well as exploring strategies for resolving conflicts in a constructive and peaceful manner.

Causes of Conflict

The causes of conflict are complex and multifaceted. Understanding these causes can help in developing effective strategies for conflict resolution. Here are some of the key causes of conflict:

1. Individual differences: No two individuals are alike in their nature, attitudes, ideals, and interests. These differences can lead to conflicts between individuals, especially when their goals, values, or interests are incompatible.

2. Cultural differences: Cultural differences among groups can cause tension and lead to conflict. Different cultural backgrounds, values, and norms can lead to misunderstandings and conflicts between individuals or groups from different cultures.

3. Clash of interests: Conflicting interests between individuals or groups can lead to conflict. For example, the interests of workers may clash with those of employers, leading to conflicts over wages, working conditions, or benefits.

4. Social change: Social change can cause cultural lag, leading to conflict. When social norms, values, or institutions change rapidly, it can create tension and conflict between those who adapt to the change and those who resist it. The parent-youth conflict is a

common example of this type of conflict.

5. Reduced supply of resources: According to Malthus, reduced supply of means of subsistence can lead to conflict. When resources are scarce, individuals or groups may compete for them, leading to conflict.

6. Innate aggression: According to Freud, the innate instinct for aggression in humans is a main cause of conflict. This perspective suggests that humans have an innate tendency towards aggression, which can manifest in conflicts.

7. Struggle for existence: According to Darwin, the principle of struggle for existence and survival of the fittest can lead to conflict. In a competitive environment, individuals or groups may struggle for resources, power, or status, leading to conflict.

8. Changing moral norms and ideas: Changes in moral norms and ideas can lead to conflicts. When societal norms and values change, it can create tension and conflict between those who support the change and those who oppose it.

9. Social disequilibrium and maladjustment: Conflicts often arise when there is social disequilibrium and maladjustment. When social institutions, norms, or values are not functioning properly, it can lead to conflicts and social unrest.

10. Differences in ideology and social norms: Conflicts can arise due to separate demands on social norms and differences of opinion on ideology. When individuals or groups have different ideological perspectives or social norms, it can lead to conflicts and disagreements.

These causes of conflict highlight the complexity and multifaceted nature of conflict. Understanding these causes can help in developing effective strategies for conflict resolution and promoting social harmony.

Functions of conflict

Conflict plays a multifaceted role in human interactions, serving both constructive and destructive purposes. On the positive side, conflict can increase solidarity and fellow feelings among groups and societies, fostering a sense of unity and cohesion. However, when conflict escalates into war or takes a hostile form, it can have devastating consequences, including loss of life, destruction of property, and profound psychological and moral impacts.

In personal relationships, conflict can also have a positive side. Verbal conflicts between friends, lovers, and married couples can clear the air, address underlying issues, and ultimately strengthen relationships. By working through conflicts, individuals can gain a deeper understanding of each other's needs, perspectives, and emotions, leading to increased empathy and intimacy.

Overall, conflict is a natural and inevitable part of human interaction, and its outcomes depend on how it is managed and resolved. By approaching conflicts in a constructive and respectful manner, individuals and groups can work towards finding solutions that promote understanding, cooperation, and growth.

According to H.T. Mazumdar, conflict can have several positive functions, including:

1. Stiffening morale and promoting solidarity: Conflict can strengthen the unity and cohesion of a group, fostering a sense of shared purpose and identity.

2. Enlargement of the victor group: When a conflict is resolved in favor of one group, it can lead to an expansion of that group's influence, power, or membership.

3. Redefining value systems: Conflict can prompt individuals and groups to re-examine their values, priorities, and principles, potentially leading to a shift in their value systems.

4. Developing non-violent techniques: Conflict can drive the development of new strategies and approaches for resolving crises peacefully, promoting non-violent conflict resolution.

5. Changing relative status: Conflict can alter the balance of power or influence between conflicting parties, potentially leading to changes in their relative status or relationships.

6. Emergence of a new consensus: Conflict can ultimately lead to a new understanding or agreement between parties, as they work towards finding a resolution and rebuilding their relationships.

These positive functions of conflict highlight its potential to drive growth, change, and improvement in individuals and groups.

Positive Consequences of Conflict

According to Lewis A. Coser, conflict can have several positive consequences, including:

1. Unity and solidarity: Conflicts between groups can bring about a higher degree of unity and solidarity within the groups, as individuals and groups come together to address a common challenge or adversary.

2. Problem identification and social readjustment: Conflict can bring problems to the surface, allowing individuals and groups to address and resolve them, ultimately leading to the readjustment of social relationships.

3. Safety-valve function: Conflict can serve as a safety-valve, allowing individuals and groups to express their frustrations and grievances, potentially preventing more severe conflicts or social unrest.

4. Achieving important goals: Conflict has been instrumental in achieving important goals, such as independence for nations and the abolition of slavery.

Other sociologists also highlight the importance of conflict in shaping society. According to Ratzenhofer, harmony and disharmony are both essential for the growth and progress of society, and conflicts are necessary to make society dynamic and progressive.

Karl Marx emphasizes the role of class conflict in protecting the interests of the exploited class and driving social change. Through class conflict, new forms of society can emerge from old forms, leading to social progress and transformation.

Mack and Young note that while conflict can result in elimination or annihilation of the opponent, most conflicts in human society end in some sort of agreement, accommodation, or fusion of opposing elements. This highlights the potential for conflict to lead to creative solutions and new relationships.

Demerits

Conflicts, whether personal or social, can have severe and far-reaching consequences. Personal conflicts can be disastrous for the individuals involved, leading to emotional distress, damaged relationships, and a decline in mental and physical well-being. They can also lower morale and weaken the solidarity of a group, causing divisions and fragmentation that can be difficult to repair.

National or social conflicts can have even more devastating effects, leading to wars between countries, loss of life, and destruction of infrastructure. Such conflicts can hinder economic progress, leading to instability, uncertainty, and a decline in economic activity. Ultimately, conflicts can cause immense human suffering, displacement, and misery, particularly for innocent civilians caught in the midst of conflict.

The negative consequences of conflicts highlight the importance of effective conflict resolution and management strategies. By understanding the causes and consequences of conflicts, individuals and groups can work towards finding peaceful and constructive solutions that promote understanding, cooperation, and social harmony.

XV
Social Change

Social change is a fundamental aspect of human society, and it is a natural process that occurs over time. The concept of social change refers to any observable difference in social phenomena, including social processes, patterns, interactions, and organization. According to various sociologists, social change can be defined as follows:

- Jones defines social change as "variations or modifications of any aspect of social processes, social patterns, social interactions, or social organization."

- Gillin and Gillin describe social change as "variations from the accepted modes of life" due to changes in geographical conditions, cultural equipment, population composition, ideologies, or other factors.

- Merrill and Andrews define social change as a situation where "a large number of persons are engaging in activities that differ from those in which they or their immediate forefathers engaged in sometime before."

- Davis views social change as "alterations that occur in social organization, that is, the structure and function of society."

- MacIver sees social change as "a process responsive to many types of change," including changes in human attitudes, beliefs, and physical environments.

Overall, social change is a complex and multifaceted phenomenon that can be driven by various factors, including technological advancements, demographic shifts, cultural exchange, and social movements. Understanding social change is essential for navigating the complexities of modern society and for promoting positive social development.

Biological Factors of Social Change

Biological factors play a significant role in shaping social change. The intermixture of biological conditions between parents results in the emergence of new biological conditions, leading to variations in each generation. This process of biological variation can lead to social changes as weaker sections are pushed out and stronger ones emerge.

The growth of population can also impact social change, as an increase in population can lead to a decline in living standards. There is a close relationship between population growth and physical health and vitality. Changes in demographic factors such as death rates, birth rates, and marriage rates can influence social attitudes and relationships.

According to MacIver and Page, changes in demographic rates are both responsive to and determinants of changes in social attitudes and relationships. For example, a society with a higher number of girls than boys may have a different system of courtship, marriage, and family organization compared to a society with a reverse demographic trend.

Overall, biological factors can have a profound impact on social change, shaping the structure and function of societies in complex ways.

Environmental Factors

The physical environment plays a significant role in shaping social conditions and governing the growth of civilization. Environmental factors can limit or permit the development of societies, influencing the rise and fall of cities, trade, and commerce. For instance, harsh environments like deserts and polar regions make it difficult for cities to develop, while more temperate climates facilitate rapid changes and growth.

The distribution of natural resources also impacts the living standards of people, with access to resources like oil, coal, and metals influencing economic development. According to MacIver and Page, every civilization exploits its environmental resources, and its continuance depends on its ability to conserve or replace these resources. Our civilization has reached a stage where it can maintain soil fertility while meeting agricultural needs, but it still faces challenges in replacing sources of power derived from oil and coal, as well as finding substitutes for essential metals like iron and copper.

The environment shapes social change by influencing the location and growth of cities, impacting trade and commerce, and shaping economic development. Ultimately, environmental factors are a crucial aspect of social change, influencing the development and growth of societies in complex ways.

Technological advancements have a profound impact on society, bringing about far-reaching and fundamental changes in our social setup. The effects of technological change can be seen in various aspects of life. Technology can improve living standards, leading to changes in class structures and standards. The rise of the middle class, the undermining of local folkways, and the disintegration of the neighborhood are all consequences of technological change.

Technological changes can also lead to the breakdown of traditional family systems, the rise of urban ways of life, and changes in the status of women. New conceptions and movements, such as communism and socialism, can emerge as a result of technological advancements. Furthermore, technological change can lead to new forms of labor organization, specialization of function, and the expansion of social contacts.

According to Ogburn, technology changes society by altering our environment, to which we adapt, often modifying customs and social institutions. MacIver and Page also note that technological change has inevitable social consequences, including the encroachment of urban influences on rural life. Overall, technological factors play a significant role in shaping social change, influencing various aspects of life and leading to the transformation of social institutions and relationships.

Cultural factors

Cultural factors play a significant role in bringing about social change. There is an intimate connection between our beliefs, valuations, and social relationships, and any change in the cultural order is accompanied by a corresponding change in the social order. The relationship between social and cultural changes is so close that it is often difficult to distinguish between the two.

In today's age of speedy and mass communication, culture crossing is more frequent and widespread. When two cultures meet and clash, social changes are inevitable. This can lead to the exchange of ideas, values, and practices, resulting in changes to social relationships and institutions. Religion, as a great cultural force, is evidently a powerful instrument for bringing about social change.

According to Kingsley Davis, no part of culture is totally unrelated to the social order. Changes in cultural branches can have a ripple effect, impacting the social system. This highlights the interconnectedness of culture and social order, and the importance of understanding the relationship between cultural factors and social change.

Overall, cultural factors are a crucial aspect of social change, shaping our social relationships, institutions, and practices in profound ways. As cultural changes occur, they can have far-reaching consequences for society, influencing the way we live, interact, and organize ourselves.

Psychological Factor in Social Change

The psychological factor plays a significant role in shaping social change. According to sociologists like Gillin and Gillin, people's attitudes, values, and beliefs influence their willingness to accept or resist change. On one hand, people tend to respect and appreciate traditional customs and practices. On the other hand, they also desire progress and innovation, and want society to be dynamic and adaptable.

When society becomes stagnant and fails to accommodate new ideas and perspectives, people may become frustrated and disillusioned. This can lead to a buildup of pressure for change, which can ultimately result in significant social transformations. In extreme cases, this frustration can boil over into revolution, as people seek to overthrow the existing social order and establish a new one.

The psychological factor is a powerful driver of social change because it influences people's motivations, attitudes, and behaviors. By understanding the psychological factors that shape human behavior, we can gain insights into the complex dynamics of social change and the ways in which people respond to changing circumstances.

Overall, the psychological factor is a crucial element in shaping social change, and its impact can be seen in the way people respond to changing social, economic, and political conditions. By recognizing the importance of psychological factors, we can better understand the complexities of social change and the ways in which people drive and respond to it.

New Ideas and Social Change

New ideas and philosophies play a significant role in shaping society and driving social change. Social reformers and political thinkers have been instrumental in introducing new ideas that challenge existing social norms and institutions.

The contributions of influential thinkers like:

- Raja Ram Mohan Roy, who advocated for social reform and women's rights

- Karl Marx, who introduced the concept of class struggle and communism

- Jawaharlal Nehru, who promoted democracy, socialism, and nationalism

- Mahatma Gandhi, who championed non-violent resistance and civil disobedience

These individuals have had a profound impact on society, inspiring change and progress through their ideas and philosophies. Their contributions have helped shape the course of history, influencing social movements, and informing policy decisions.

New ideas can challenge existing power structures, promote social justice, and inspire collective action, ultimately leading to significant social changes. By introducing new perspectives and challenging existing norms, social reformers and political thinkers can help create a more just and equitable society.

Population factors

Changes in population characteristics, such as size and quality, can significantly impact social organization, customs, traditions, institutions, and associations. Demographic shifts can influence social relationships, economic institutions, and societal norms. For instance, an increase or decrease in population can affect economic institutions and social relationships, while a change in the ratio of men to women can impact marriage patterns, family structures, and the status of women in society.

The age distribution of a population, including the proportion of young and old individuals, can also shape social relationships, economic opportunities, and societal values. Furthermore, birth and death rates can influence population growth, age distribution, and social institutions. These demographic changes can have far-reaching consequences, impacting family structures, economic opportunities, and social interactions.

Overall, population factors play a significant role in shaping social change, and understanding these dynamics is essential for addressing the challenges and opportunities that arise from demographic shifts. By recognizing the impact of population changes, we can better navigate the complexities of social change and work towards creating a more adaptable and resilient society.

Economic Factors and Social Change

Economic factors have long been recognized as a significant driver of social change. Thinkers such as Machi, Karl Marx, and others have argued that economic conditions shape society and influence social relationships. The institutions of production, distribution, exchange, and control over wealth all play a vital role in shaping social dynamics.

Impact of Economic Factors

Economic factors can impact society in various ways, including:

- Influencing population characteristics: Economic conditions can affect the physical and mental well-being of individuals, leading to differences between the rich and the poor.

- Shaping vital social processes: Economic factors can influence birth and death rates, as well as other social processes.

- Impact on crime and migration: Economic conditions can contribute to crime, suicide, and migration patterns.

- Determining social organization: Economic factors can shape the form of social organization and drive social change.

- Influencing religious institutions: Economic conditions can impact religious institutions and people's attitudes towards religion.

- Triggering social unrest: Economic factors can lead to strikes, lock-outs, and violent demonstrations, which can decay political organizations.

Karl Marx and Economic Determinism

Karl Marx is a key figure in the discussion of economic factors and social change. According to Marx, economic conditions are the primary driver of social change, shaping the relationships between individuals and classes. Marx's ideas highlight the significance of economic factors in understanding social dynamics and change.

Overall, economic factors play a crucial role in shaping society and driving social change. Understanding the impact of economic conditions can help us better navigate the complexities of social change and work towards creating a more equitable society.

Nature of Social Change

Social change is a complex and multifaceted phenomenon that affects all societies, regardless of their level of development or cultural background. The nature of social change can be understood through several key characteristics:

1. Universality: Social change is a universal phenomenon that occurs in all societies, whether primitive or civilized. Every society undergoes change in response to internal and external factors.

2. Community Change: Social change is a change that occurs in the life of the entire community, rather than just individual members. It involves shifts in social structures, institutions, and relationships.

3. Variable Speed: The speed of social change is not uniform and can vary significantly between different societies and contexts. For example, social change in urban areas tends to be faster than in rural areas due to differences in exposure to new ideas, technologies, and economic opportunities.

4. Time Factor: The nature and speed of social change are affected by and related to the time factor. The speed of social change can differ significantly from one age to another, with modern times often experiencing more rapid change due to advancements in technology and communication.

5. Natural and Inevitable: Social change occurs as an essential law of nature. Change is a natural part of human societies, and social change is an inevitable aspect of this process. Societies adapt and evolve over time in response to changing circumstances.

6. Unpredictability: Definite prediction of social change is not possible, as there is no inherent law of social change that would assume definite forms. Social change is often the result of complex interactions between various factors, making it difficult to predict with certainty.

7. Chain-Reaction Sequence: Social change often shows a chain-reaction sequence, where one change leads to another. For example, industrialization can lead to urbanization, which in turn can lead to changes in family structures and social relationships.

8. Multiple Factors: Social change results from the interaction of a number of factors, including economic, cultural, political, and technological influences. These factors can interact in complex ways, leading to diverse outcomes.

9. Modification and Replacement: Social changes can take the form of modification or replacement. For example, changes in food habits or technological advancements can lead to new forms of social behavior, while old practices may be replaced by new ones.

10. Dynamic Process: Social change is a dynamic process that involves the replacement of old orders with new ones, leading to a continuous transformation of societies. This process can be driven by various factors, including technological innovations, social movements, and changes in values and beliefs.

Overall, social change is a complex and multifaceted phenomenon that is shaped by a variety of factors and can have far-reaching consequences for individuals and societies. Understanding the nature of social change can help us better navigate the challenges and opportunities that arise from it.

Theory of Deterioration

The Theory of Deterioration is a perspective on social change that suggests that society is gradually deteriorating over time. According to this theory, humans originally lived in a perfect state of happiness, often referred to as a "golden age." However, with the passage of time, society has been declining, and people are moving further away from this ideal state.

Key Features

- Pessimistic View: This theory takes a pessimistic view of social change, seeing it as a process of decline and deterioration.

- Mythological Support: Proponents of this theory often draw on mythological accounts of a past golden age to support their arguments.

- Inevitable Decline: According to this theory, social change is driven by an inevitable process of decline, which cannot be halted or reversed.

Implications

The Theory of Deterioration has implications for how people understand and respond to social change. It can lead to a sense of nostalgia for a past era and a skepticism towards efforts to bring about positive change in the present.

Overall, the Theory of Deterioration is one perspective on social change that highlights the complexities and challenges of understanding and addressing social transformation.

Cyclic Theory of Social Change

The Cyclic Theory of Social Change posits that societies and civilizations undergo cycles of growth, decline, and eventual decay. This theory is supported by various scholars, including Oswald Spengler, Vilfredo Pareto, and Arnold J. Toynbee, who have analyzed the rise and fall of major civilizations throughout history.

Key Features

- Cycles of Growth and Decline: Societies and civilizations are seen as going through cycles of growth, maturity, and eventual decline.

- Historical Patterns: The theory is based on the study of historical patterns and the rise and fall of civilizations such as the Egyptian, Roman, and Greek civilizations.

- Stages of Societal Development: According to Arnold J. Toynbee, societies pass through three stages:

1. Response to Challenge: Societies respond to challenges and grow through creative solutions.

2. Time of Trouble: Societies face internal and external challenges that lead to instability and conflict.

3. Gradual Degeneration: Societies eventually decline and degenerate due to internal decay and external pressures.

Implications

The Cyclic Theory of Social Change suggests that societies are subject to natural cycles of growth and decline, and that these cycles are inevitable. This theory can help us understand the dynamics of social change and the factors that contribute to the rise and fall of civilizations.

Linear Theory of Social Change

The Linear Theory of Social Change, as proposed by Auguste Comte, suggests that societies progress through a series of stages in a linear fashion. Comte identified three stages of societal development:

Stages of Societal Development

1. Theological Stage: In this stage, people believe that supernatural powers control and design the world. Societies in this stage often attribute natural phenomena to divine intervention.

2. Metaphysical Stage: In this stage, people begin to abstract and generalize about the world, moving away from supernatural explanations. They seek to explain social behavior through abstract concepts and philosophical ideas.

3. Positive Stage: In this stage, societies focus on empirical observation and scientific study. People seek to understand the world through evidence-based knowledge and rational inquiry.

Key Features

- Linear Progression: Comte's theory suggests that societies progress through these stages in a linear fashion, with each stage building on the previous one.

- Evolution of Knowledge: The theory emphasizes the evolution of human knowledge and understanding, from supernatural to abstract to scientific.

Implications

The Linear Theory of Social Change highlights the importance of understanding the progression of human knowledge and societal development. It suggests that societies can advance through the adoption of scientific and rational methods of inquiry.

Herbert Spencer's Theory of Social Change

Herbert Spencer's theory of social change is based on the analogy of an organism. He believed that societies evolve and change in a manner similar to living organisms.

Key Features

- Militant Society: Spencer described early societies as being characterized by conflict and struggle for existence, with different groups competing for resources and power.

- Industrial Society: As societies evolve, they transition to industrialism, which is marked by increased differentiation and specialization.

- Integration: Spencer believed that the next stage of social evolution involves integration, where different groups and institutions come together to form a cohesive whole.

Social Evolution

Spencer's theory suggests that social change is driven by the process of evolution, where societies adapt and change in response to their environment. He saw this process as being driven by the struggle for existence and the survival of the fittest.

Implications

Spencer's theory has implications for understanding social change and the evolution of societies. It highlights the importance of adaptation and competition in shaping social institutions and relationships.

Karl Marx's Theory of Social Change

Karl Marx's theory of social change emphasizes the role of economic factors and conditions in shaping society. According to Marx, changes in the mode of production and exchange are the ultimate causes of social changes and revolutions. He believed that economic factors are the primary drivers of social change, and that class struggle between different economic groups is the engine of historical progress.

Marx identified five stages of societal development: oriental, ancient, feudal, capitalistic, and communistic. He argued that each stage is characterized by a unique economic order, and that the transition from one stage to another is driven by class struggle. Marx believed that capitalism would eventually give way to socialism, and ultimately, communism. In a communist society, there would be no state, no class, no conflict, and no exploitation. The principle of communism would be "from each according to his capacities, to each according to his needs."

According to Marx, the transition to communism would involve two stages. The first stage would be a dictatorship of the proletariat, during which the working class would rule despotically and crush out all remnants of capitalism. The second stage would be real communism, where there would be no state, no class, and no conflict. Marx envisioned a society in which the social order would have reached a state of perfection, where people would be free to develop their full potential without the constraints of class and economic exploitation.

However, Marx's theory has been subject to criticism and challenge from other social thinkers. Some argue that non-material elements of culture, such as religion, are more important drivers of social change. Thinkers like Gustave Le Bon, George Sorel, James G. Frazer, and Max Weber have highlighted the role of religion in shaping social change, citing examples such as the emergence of Hinduism, Islam, Christianity, and Judaism. These thinkers argue that economic or material phenomena are subordinate to non-material factors, and that religion has played a significant role in shaping human history and society.

Overall, Marx's theory remains a significant contribution to understanding social change, but its limitations and criticisms have led to ongoing debates and discussions in the field of sociology. Despite these debates, Marx's ideas continue to influence contemporary thought and action, and his theory remains an important part of the sociological canon.

Theory of Systematic Efforts

The Theory of Systematic Efforts is a perspective on social change that emphasizes the role of human agency and deliberate action in shaping society. This theory suggests that social change can be brought about by conscious and systematic efforts, rather than relying solely on chance or unplanned events. By harnessing the power of knowledge, education, and rational planning, individuals and societies can drive meaningful change and improve their circumstances.

Key Proponents

The Theory of Systematic Efforts is supported by thinkers such as Ludwig Stein and Hobhouse, who argue that deliberate and planned actions can lead to significant social change.

Key Points

- Conscious Efforts: Social change can be driven by intentional and planned actions.

- Spread of Knowledge and Literacy: Education and knowledge play a crucial role in enabling effective planning and decision-making.

- Intellect over Emotions: Through education and knowledge, intellect can assert itself over emotions, leading to more informed and rational decision-making.

- Planned Efforts: Conscious efforts in a planned way are more effective in bringing about social change than unplanned and unsystematic efforts.

Implications

The Theory of Systematic Efforts suggests that social change can be accelerated and made more effective through deliberate and planned actions. This theory highlights the importance of education, knowledge, and rational decision-making in driving social progress. By adopting a systematic and intentional approach to social change, individuals and societies can create positive and lasting impact.

Structural-Factor Theory

The Structural-Factor Theory is a sociological perspective that seeks to understand social change by examining the underlying structures and relationships within society. This theory posits that social change is driven by changes in the functions and relationships between different social institutions, systems, and structures. By analyzing the complex web of relationships between social functions, the Structural-Factor Theory provides insights into the dynamics of social change and the ways in which societies evolve over time.

Key Proponents

The Structural-Factor Theory is supported by prominent sociologists such as Talcott Parsons and Robert K. Merton, who have contributed significantly to our understanding of social structures and their role in shaping social change.

Key Points

- Interdependence of Social Functions: Each function of society directly and positively influences others, making every social function complementary.

- Changes in Functions: Changes in social functions are seen as the reasons behind social change.

- No Exclusive Functions: Every social function is interconnected and interdependent, with no function being exclusive or isolated.

Implications

The Structural-Factor Theory highlights the importance of understanding the complex relationships between different social functions. By recognizing the interdependence of social functions, individuals and societies can better anticipate and respond to changes, ultimately driving positive social change. This theory provides a valuable framework for analyzing social change and understanding the dynamics of social systems.

Pluralistic Theory

The Pluralistic Theory is a perspective on social change that emphasizes the complexity and multifaceted nature of social phenomena. This theory posits that social change is not the result of a single factor, but rather the outcome of multiple factors interacting and combining in complex ways.

Key Points

- Multiple Causes: Social change is driven by a combination of factors, including materialistic, non-materialistic, cultural, and technological influences.

- Collective Impact: The collective impact of various factors leads to social change, rather than a single factor dominating the process.

- Complexity: Social change is a complex and multifaceted phenomenon that cannot be reduced to a single cause or factor.

Implications

The Pluralistic Theory highlights the importance of considering multiple perspectives and factors when analyzing social change. By recognizing the complexity of social phenomena, individuals and societies can develop a more nuanced understanding of the forces driving social change and develop more effective strategies for addressing social issues.

XVI

Sociology of Legal Profession

The sociology of legal profession is a fascinating field of study that explores the complex dynamics of the legal profession and its impact on society. Law is a fundamental institution that shapes our social, economic, and political lives, and the legal profession plays a crucial role in interpreting and applying the law. Sociologists examine the legal profession as a social institution, analyzing its structure, functions, and impact on society.

The legal profession is a unique occupation that requires specialized knowledge, skills, and ethics. Lawyers, judges, and other legal professionals play a vital role in upholding the rule of law, protecting individual rights, and promoting justice. However, the legal profession is not immune to social, economic, and cultural influences that shape its practices, norms, and values.

By applying sociological perspectives to the study of the legal profession, we can gain a deeper understanding of the complex dynamics at play and how they impact society. This includes examining the social context in which the legal profession operates, the impact of law on society, and the role of legal professionals in shaping the law and its application.

Definition and Importance of Law

- Law as an instrument of society: Law is a tool used by society to achieve justice, stability, and peaceful change.

- Principles of law: Law is based on principles recognized or enforced by public and regular tribunals in the administration of justice.

- Role of legal professionals: Legal professionals, such as lawyers and judges, play a vital role in upholding the interests of justice and ensuring the administration of justice.

Characteristics of the Legal Profession

- Skilled occupation: The legal profession requires specialized knowledge and skills in jurisprudence, court practice, and matters affecting rights and obligations.

- Principles of honor: Legal professionals are expected to adhere to principles of honor and ethics in their practice.

- Education and qualification: Legal professionals typically undergo extensive education and training to qualify for their role.

Role of Sociologists in Understanding the Legal Profession

- Analyzing the social context: Sociologists study the social context in which the legal profession operates, including the impact of social norms, values, and power dynamics.

- Understanding the impact of law on society: Sociologists examine how law shapes society and how society shapes law, including the role of legal professionals in this process.

- Identifying issues and challenges: Sociologists identify issues and challenges facing the legal profession, such as access to justice, diversity, and ethics.

Eligibility for legal profession.-Advocates only are entitled to practice in law courts. An advocate has to enroll in any State Bar Council. A person is qualified to be admitted as an advocate on a State roll, if he fulfils the following five conditions:-

i. He is a citizen of India.

i. He has completed the age of 21 years.

iii. He has obtained a degree in law from any university under law.

iv. He fulfils such other conditions as may be specified in the rules made by the State Bar Council.

v. He has paid, in respect of the enrolment stamp duty and an enrolment fee payable to the State Bar Council.

After taking an oath in Bar Council, he will be admitted as an advocate. Definition of Sociology of Legal Profession

Now, "Sociology of Legal Profession" may be defined as a study or science of institutions dealing with legal phenomena, the interconnection of different parties in legal system and the interdependence of groups of jural life.

Legal Professional Organization: Bar Council of India

The Bar Council of India and the State Bar Councils are constituted as per the Advocates Act, 1961. They are statutory bodies. They are organised by the periodically elected body consisting of a Chairman, Vice-Chairman and members of Executive. Every Bar Council shall be a body corporate having perpetual succession and a common seal, with power to acquire and hold property, both movable and immovable, and to contract, and may by the name by which it is known to sue and be sued. The functions of the Bar Council o India are:

i. to lay down standards of professional conduct and etiquette for advocates;

(ii) to lay down the procedure to be followed by itsdisciplinary committee; (iii) to safeguard the rights, privileges and interests of advocates;

iv. to promote and support law reform;

v. to deal with and dispose of any matter arising under the Advocates Act, 1961;

vi. to exercise general supervision and control over State Bar Council;

vii. to promote legal education;

viii. to recognise universities whose degree in law shall be a qualification for enrolment as an advocate;

ix. to conduct seminars and organise talks on legal topics by eminent jurists;

x. to organise legal aid to the poor;

xi. to recognise on a reciprocal basis foreign qualifications in law obtained outside India;

xii. to manage and invest the funds of the Bar Council;

xiii. to prove for the election of its members;

xiv. to perform all other functions conferred on it or under the Advocates Act, 1961.

The Bar Council consists of different elected committees such as Executive Committee for 2 years, Disciplinary Committee for 3 years, Legal Education Committee for 4 years, Legal Aid Executive Committee for 2 years, Advocates Fund Committee for 2 years, etc.

Introduction to Legal Literacy and Awareness

Legal literacy and awareness are essential components of a just and equitable society. In today's complex legal landscape, individuals need to be aware of their rights, privileges, and obligations to navigate the system effectively. Legal literacy empowers individuals to make informed decisions, access justice, and claim their entitlements. Moreover, it promotes social justice, equality, and human rights, enabling individuals to participate actively in the democratic process.

The importance of legal literacy cannot be overstated. Ignorance of the law is no excuse, and individuals who are unaware of their rights and obligations are more likely to be exploited or marginalized. Legal literacy camps and programs play a vital role in educating people about the law, its applications, and its implications. These initiatives help bridge the knowledge gap, especially for vulnerable populations, and promote access to justice.

Objectives of Legal Literacy Camps

- Educating weaker sections: Legal literacy camps aim to educate weaker sections of society about their rights, benefits, and privileges guaranteed by social welfare legislations and enactments.

- Promoting dispute resolution: These camps also encourage the settlement of disputes through Lok Adalats, promoting alternative dispute resolution mechanisms.

- Spreading legal awareness: Legal Services Authorities take measures to spread legal literacy and awareness among people, focusing on weaker sections of society.

Role of Stakeholders

- Law graduate students: Law graduate students participate in legal literacy camps, providing legal knowledge and awareness to the masses.

- Members of Bar Councils: Members of Bar Councils contribute to legal literacy camps, sharing their expertise and experience with the community.

- Judges: Judges participate in legal literacy camps, providing insights into the legal system and promoting access to justice.

Impact of Legal Literacy Camps

- Empowering individuals: Legal literacy camps empower individuals with knowledge of their rights and privileges, enabling them to make informed decisions and access justice.

- Promoting social justice: By educating people about their rights and benefits, legal literacy camps promote social justice and equality.

- Encouraging community participation: Legal literacy camps foster community participation in promoting justice and rule of law, encouraging people to take an active role in shaping their legal environment.

Conclusion

Legal literacy and awareness are crucial for promoting justice, equality, and human rights in society. By organizing legal literacy camps and promoting legal awareness, Legal Services Authorities play a vital role in empowering individuals and communities, promoting social justice, and upholding the rule of law.

Objectives of Legal Literacy Camps

The legal literacy camps are designed to achieve several key objectives, including:

1. Awareness

- Acquiring awareness of rights: To help social groups and individuals acquire an awareness of their rights, privileges, and benefits.

- Sensitivity to laws: To sensitize people to the laws applicable to them, enabling them to understand their legal entitlements.

- Understanding legal frameworks: To educate people about the legal frameworks that govern their lives, including laws related to education, employment, health, and social welfare.

2. Knowledge

- Gaining experiences and understanding: To help social groups and individuals gain a variety of experiences and acquire a basic understanding of law that is helpful in solving their problems.

- Practical application: To enable people to apply their knowledge of law in practical situations, promoting self-reliance and empowerment.

- Access to justice: To educate people about the procedures and processes involved in accessing justice, including the role of courts, tribunals, and other dispute resolution mechanisms.

3. Attitude

- Empowering individuals: To awaken individuals from a meek surrendering nature before the superior class and change their attitude to fight injustice done to them legally.

- Fighting injustice: To empower people to challenge injustice and promote a culture of rights-based activism.

- Promoting social change: To promote social change by empowering people to demand their rights and challenge unjust laws and practices.

4. Participation

- Utilizing legal aid: To make people aware of the legal aid available to them and encourage them to utilize it to fight against injustice.

- Promoting access to justice: To promote access to justice and ensure that people are able to navigate the legal system effectively.

- Encouraging community involvement: To encourage community involvement in promoting legal literacy and awareness, including the participation of local leaders, NGOs, and other stakeholders.

Conducting Legal Literacy Camps

The Legal Service Authorities play a crucial role in conducting legal literacy camps, particularly in areas where rural people, depressed class people, and other vulnerable populations live. These camps are designed to:

- Create awareness: Create awareness about various laws and legal entitlements among people.

- Involve NGOs: Involve non-governmental organizations (NGOs) to participate and help in conducting the legal literacy camps.

- Use effective methods: Use effective methods to convey legal information, including interactive sessions, role-playing, and visual aids.

Impact of Legal Literacy Camps

The impact of legal literacy camps can be significant, including:

- Empowering individuals: Empowering individuals with knowledge of their rights and entitlements.

- Promoting social justice: Promoting social justice by challenging unjust laws and practices.

- Improving access to justice: Improving access to justice by educating people about the procedures and processes involved in accessing justice.

By achieving these objectives, legal literacy camps can play a vital role in promoting legal awareness, empowering individuals, and promoting social justice.

The Constitution of India, through Article 39-A, ensures equal justice and free legal aid to citizens who are economically poor or have other disabilities. This provision recognizes the importance of access to justice for all, regardless of socio-economic status. To implement this provision, several laws and regulations have been enacted, including the Civil Procedure Code, Criminal Procedure Code, and the Advocates Act, 1961.

The Legal Services Authorities Act, 1987, is a significant legislation that provides for the establishment of legal services authorities at the national, state, and district levels. These authorities are responsible for providing free legal aid to the poor and needy. The National Legal Services Authority (NALSA) is the apex body that oversees the implementation of legal aid programs across the country.

The legal services authorities provide a range of services, including legal advice, representation in court, and mediation. They also organize legal literacy camps and awareness programs to educate people about their rights and entitlements. A Legal Aid Fund has been established to meet the expenditure required for providing free legal aid to the poor and needy.

The provision of legal aid has a significant impact on promoting access to justice. It empowers the poor and weaker sections of society to claim their rights and challenge injustice. By providing legal aid, the legal services authorities promote social justice and reduce inequality. They ensure that all citizens have equal access to justice, regardless of their socio-economic status.

Overall, the legal aid system in India is an important mechanism for promoting access to justice and upholding the principles of equality and fairness enshrined in the Constitution. It plays a vital role in empowering the poor and vulnerable sections of society and promoting social justice.

The following persons who have to file or defend a case shall be entitled to free legal services:-

i.   a member of a Scheduled Caste or Scheduled Tribes; or

ii. a victim of trafficking in human beings or
iii. a woman or a child; or

iv. a person with disability; or

v.   a person under circumstances to the underserved want such as being a victim of a mass disaster, ethnic violence, caste atrocity, flood, drought, earthquake or industrial disaster; or

vi. an industrial workman; or

vii. in custody, including custody in a protective home or in a juvenile home or in a psychiatric hospital or psychiatric nursing home; or

viii. in receipt of annual income less than rupees nine thousand or such other higher amount as may be prescribed by the State Government.

The sociology of the legal profession examines the complex dynamics of the legal profession, including its organizations, relationships, and services. This field of study helps us understand how legal professionals interact with each other, with their clients, and with the broader society. It explores the role of professional organizations, such as bar associations and law societies, in shaping the legal profession. Additionally, it investigates the relationships between lawyers, judges, clients, and other stakeholders in the legal system, as well as the services provided by legal professionals to individuals, businesses, and society. By studying the sociology of the legal profession, we can gain insights into the ways in which the legal system shapes society and how society shapes the legal system.